MAP LEGEND

Expressway	⊖	Shop/ Shopping	⊡	Embassy/Consulate
Major Street	B	Bank		Theater
Secondary Street	⊠	Post Office	✸	Police
Large Minor Street	School	✚	Hospital
Small Minor Street	■	University		Stadium
Footpath	Ⓐ	Apartment	❶	Tourist Information
Parks/Gardens	⛩	Shinto Shrine	Ⓗ	Hotel
One-way Arrow	卍	Buddhist Temple	Ⓡ	Restaurant
Bus Terminal	†	Church	★	Place of Interest
Travel Agent/Airline Office			🏛	Museum

Published by Tuttle Publishing, an imprint of Periplus Editions (HK) Ltd

www.tuttlepublishing.com

Copyright © 2015 by Periplus Editions (HK) Ltd
Photo Credits on page 96

ISBN 978-4-8053-0964-3

Distributed by

North America, Latin America & Europe
Tuttle Publishing
364 Innovation Drive
North Clarendon, VT 05759-9436 U.S.A.
Tel: 1 (802) 773-8930;Fax: 1 (802) 773-6993
info@tuttlepublishing.com
www.tuttlepublishing.com

Japan
Tuttle Publishing
Yaekari Building, 3rd Floor
5-4-12 Osaki, Shinagawa-ku, Tokyo 141 0032
Tel: (81) 3 5437-0171;Fax: (81) 3 5437-0755
sales@ tuttle.co.jp
www.tuttle.co.jp

Asia Pacific
Berkeley Books Pte. Ltd.
61 Tai Seng Avenue #02-12, Singapore 534167
Tel: (65) 6280-1330; Fax: (65) 6280-6290
inquiries@periplus.com.sg
www.periplus.com

20 19 18 17 16   10 9 8 7 6 5 4 3

Printed in China   1607RR

Getting Around

KYOTO

and NARA

POCKET ATLAS
AND TRANSPORTATION GUIDE

Includes Nara, Fushimi, Uji, Mt Hiei,
Lake Biwa, Ohara and Kurama

Colin Smith

TUTTLE Publishing

Tokyo | Rutland, Vermont | Singapore

CONTENTS

Left: *Ginkaku-ji Temple*

Introducing Kyoto

The Capital of Japan for 1,000 Years and Still Its Cultural Heartland

Kyoto was the imperial capital of Japan for over 1,000 years and it is still known as the heartland of the country's traditions and aesthetics. A small city compared to Tokyo, it nonetheless attracts tens of millions of visitors a year. Along with the nearby city of Nara, Japan's capital in even more ancient times, Kyoto is the timeless yin to Tokyo's hectic, hyper-urban yang. Its narrow alleys, temples and cultural treasures provide the ideal counterpoint to cyber-cute "Cool Japan" and make the city an essential destination for overseas travelers seeking a full experience of the country.

About This Book

The public transportation system is another aspect of Kyoto that makes it radically different from the Tokyo region. While Tokyo boasts the most extensive and efficient transit network in the world, Kyoto had no subways at all until 30 years ago, and even now has only two subway lines. The grid layout of the city is not a strategy to facilitate modern commerce, like in New York, but a preservation of the original 8th-century town plan modeled on those of T'ang Dynasty China. Labyrinthine underground passages and snarls of elevated roads, features of most Japanese cities, are pleasantly absent, but so is the convenience of zooming from anywhere to anywhere on assorted subways, railways and highways. Getting around smoothly is a matter of knowing the basic layout of the city, navigating the bus network, walking or taking cabs to closer destinations and, at times, a larger helping of patience than Japan's more contemporary cities require.

Even here, public transportation is much more dependable and punctual than in most parts of the world and it is not necessary to speak Japanese. However, your visit will be much more enriching and enjoyable if you know where to go, the best way to get there and the quickest way back. This pocket atlas and transportation guide provides all the information you need in order to navigate Kyoto as well as Nara and other nearby attractions. It starts with getting to Kyoto on an international or domestic flight or by ground transportation; continues with a look at the various areas of Kyoto, what to see there and how to get there and get around; explores the benefits and drawbacks of the many transport options, and gives all the inside information, tips and know-how you need to navigate the system properly, along with extensive route maps, schematic diagrams and area maps. In addition to the more common modes of transport, there are explanations of lesser-known possibilities like hiring a sightseeing taxi or renting a bicycle for the day.

Kyoto and Beyond

Those who are staying for more than a couple of days in Kyoto will want to consider taking a day trip or two outside the city. In addition to the historic city of Nara, there are the mountains that encircle Kyoto; scenic Lake Biwa, the largest lake in Japan; and rustic, romantic villages in the region that are surprisingly easy to reach. Details of these getaways are included in the book along with a full range of maps.

Thanks to all the comfortable and reliable transport options and the fascinating roadside and rail-side scenery, getting around can be half the fun on a trip to Japan as long as you have the necessary information at your fingertips. Enjoy the journey.

Left: *Tourists in old Kyoto*

Arriving in Kyoto by Air and by Train and Getting to Kyoto from the Airports

Kyoto is not a large city and most travelers enter it via the same portal, **Kyoto Station**, in the south-central area of the city, south of the Imperial Palace. From here, a variety of buses, trains and taxis can take you to your final destination. If you're just arriving in Japan, you must first get to Kyoto from the airport, which is a fair distance away. This section of the book covers arrival at the airport, transport from the airport to Kyoto Station, and how to reach your accommodations from the station.

If arriving in Kyoto from elsewhere in Japan, you will also most likely arrive at Kyoto Station, but even from other major train or bus stations the same basic rules apply: municipal buses and taxis are the main modes of transport. Buses are much cheaper but more confusing and time-consuming, whereas taxis are pricier but much more convenient, especially for those with lots of luggage. Subways or commuter trains might also be a good option, depending on where you're going.

Arriving at Kansai International Airport

Kansai International Airport (Kansai Airport for short) is the main international airport serving the Kansai region, which includes Kyoto, Osaka, Kobe and Nara. Located about 80 km (about 50 miles) south of Kyoto, it's a newer, sparkling clean and orderly airport that makes a pleasant introduction to Japan.

However, for a major international flight hub, Kansai Airport is served by relatively few airlines and some travelers' itineraries will have them flying to another city such as Tokyo and transferring to a brief domestic flight to **Osaka Itami Airport** instead. Officially known as Osaka International Airport, it's nonetheless domestic and smaller than Kansai. At about 40 km (about 25 miles) away, Itami is the closest airport to Kyoto. Recently constructed **Kobe Airport**, the third airport serving the Kansai region, is a smaller domestic airport

that's also within reasonable distance of Kyoto although it primarily serves the city of Kobe.

After Kansai, the nearest major international airport is Central Japan International Airport (Centrair) in Nagoya, about 110 km (about 70 miles) to the east. Though not much farther distance-wise from Kyoto than Kansai International Airport, Centrair primarily serves the Chubu region of Japan centered on Nagoya and doesn't offer very convenient access to Kyoto.

At just about any Japanese airport, visitors arriving for the first time will be impressed by the cleanliness, courtesy and efficiency. Japanese airports regularly earn high marks in world airport rankings, and in the 2009 Skytrax World Airport Awards, Kansai Airport earned the top prize in the category "Cleanest Airport Washrooms"!

Getting to Kyoto from Kansai Airport

From Kansai Airport, there are a number of ways to reach Kyoto.

Limousine buses leave from in front of the passenger terminal building, take 90–120 minutes and cost ¥2,500 per adult (¥4,000 for a round-trip ticket), children half price. Buses run every 45 minutes or so and arrive at the Hachijo East entrance on the southeast corner of Kyoto Station. The advantage of the limousine bus is that it's easy to use. Simply buy a ticket from a machine outside the passenger terminal just steps away from customs, wait in line for the bus, turn over your luggage to an attendant and receive a claim stub, and give your ticket to the driver when you get on. The disadvantages are that it can take a while if there's traffic, and leaves you at Kyoto Station where you will then have to reach your accommodations by other means.

Trains take less time than buses and are more predictable as they nearly always run strictly on time and are not affected by traffic. The **JR (Japan Rail) Haruka rapid express** takes about 75 minutes to reach Kyoto Station, costs about ¥3,000 and departs every half hour or so from **Kansai Airport Station**, directly connected to the airport. (Follow the signs or ask at an information counter.) It might be a more pleasant ride than the bus but it's a bit more expensive and you will have to handle your own luggage.

There are also other **JR Kansai Airport Rapid Service** trains to Osaka or Kyobashi stations in Osaka from which you can transfer to other trains that might put you closer to your accommodations than Haruka does (see train map, pages 12–13). These are advised only for travelers who have some experience of the Japanese rail system and who don't have a lot of luggage or young children with them.

Yasaka Taxi runs a door-to-door **Kansai Airport Shuttle** service from around 7.30 am to 9 pm. This is a shared mini-bus taxi with a maximum capacity of nine people, which at ¥3,500 per adult (children under 6 on laps free, children under 12 half price,

students and seniors ¥3,000) is only a bit more expensive than the bus or train and will take you directly to your accommodations. They will also take you back to the airport when you depart. One large piece of luggage per person, plus carry-on bag, is free, with a ¥1,000 surcharge for additional large bags. Reservations must be made at least two days in advance: call +81-75-803-4800 or visit the Yasaka Taxi website: www.yasaka.jp/english/shuttle/.

Another company, **MK Taxi**, runs a service similar in both prices and particulars. Unlike Yasaka, their **MK Skygate Shuttle** service serves Osaka Itami Airport as well for ¥2,300 per person. Make reservations at least two days in advance at +81-75-778-5489 (9 am–6 pm) or online at www.mk-group.co.jp/english/shuttle/.

Both of these companies have counters right near the south exit of the International Arrivals lobby at Kansai Airport, which you will enter

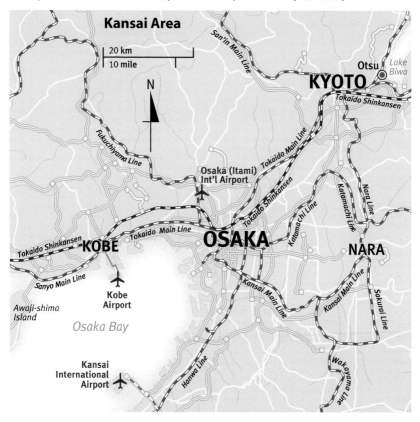

after clearing customs. It should be noted that they will not go to certain more out-of-the-way areas, and if your flight is considerably delayed they will leave without you as there will be other passengers sharing the ride. These points aside, this is an attractive option, especially for those with large families or lots of luggage. Just be sure to make reservations in advance.

Arriving at Osaka International (Itami) Airport

If you are flying from elsewhere in Japan and arriving at Osaka Itami Airport, the options are similar. **Osaka Airport Limousine buses** to Kyoto Station depart from bus stop no. 5 outside the north terminal and bus stop no. 15 outside the south terminal. Buses take about 50 minutes and cost ¥1,280 (purchase tickets from a vending machine). They run from about 8 am to 9 pm.

If you arrive early in the morning or late at night, trains (running from around 6 am to midnight) are an option, but there are none directly to Kyoto. You must take the **Osaka**

Monorail to **Hotarugaike Station** and change to the **Hankyu Kyoto Line**. MK Taxi also operates shuttles from Osaka Itami Airport. (For contact details, see page 7.)

From any airport or major train station, **normal taxis** are available 24 hours a day. These will be more expensive though most offer flat fares from the airports to Kyoto Station, which are a good deal cheaper than a normal metered fare would be. A reasonable fare would be about ¥13,000-¥15,000 from Kansai Airport and around ¥9,000 from Osaka Itami Airport. Taxis can be found near the limousine bus stands outside the passenger terminal at Kansai or Osaka Itami airports.

Arriving at Kobe and Nagoya Airports

Another smaller domestic airport in the region is Kobe Airport. It's a little farther away from Kyoto and doesn't have the limousine bus or mini-bus taxi services that Kansai and Osaka airports have. However, it is feasible to reach Kyoto by train. Take the **Port Liner**

Shinkansen Train Lines

train (directly connected to the airport terminal) to **Sannomiya** in Kobe and change to the **JR Kyoto Line** to Kyoto Station. It takes about 100 minutes and costs around ¥1,400.

Getting to Kyoto from Central Japan International Airport (Centrair) in Nagoya is time-consuming as one must first get from the airport to **Nagoya Station** and then on to Kyoto. If entering Japan at this airport, people traveling to Kyoto may want to take a connecting flight to an airport in the Kansai region. Otherwise, the best way to reach Kyoto is by taking the **Meitetsu (Nagoya Railroad)** and **JR trains** to Nagoya Station, then boarding a **Shinkansen** (high-speed train) for Kyoto.

Getting to Kyoto from Elsewhere in Japan

If you're traveling to Kyoto from elsewhere in Japan, it's a good idea to take the high-speed **Shinkansen** "bullet train," if possible. From Tokyo and Nagoya in the east or Hiroshima and Kyushu in the west, reaching Kyoto by Shinkansen is comparable in speed and cost to flying but delivers you directly to Kyoto Station rather than at an airport some distance from the city. It's also a quintessential Japanese experience that you will enjoy unless it's during an extended national holiday when they become very crowded. These come three times a year: at the end of April through the first week of May, in mid-August and at New Year.

To buy a ticket for the Shinkansen, go to the station's **JR ticket office** (which has a green color scheme) or use a machine in some stations. There are reserved and non-reserved seats. Non-reserved seats cost slightly less and also have the advantage of not requiring you to take a train at a particular time (they leave every five or ten minutes as a rule, so don't worry if you miss one). Reserved seats will guarantee you more space around you unless it's one of the aforementioned extended national holidays.

Only major cities have Shinkansen service. If you're coming from somewhere off the beaten path, you will be on a regular, non-"bullet" train, but most likely you will arrive at the same place, namely Kyoto Station. This is really Kyoto's only major transportation hub and **intercity buses** arrive there as well. These are the cheapest mode of transport but are not worth the trouble unless you're really on a shoestring. From Tokyo to Kyoto, for example, to save ¥5,000 or so you will spend at least five hours longer than on the Shinkansen and in considerably less comfort.

Getting from Kyoto Station to Your Hotel

Taxis, including the mini-bus taxis from the airport, can take you directly to your accommodations or at least nearby but most trains and buses will drop you off at **Kyoto Station**. This is a massive, modernist cube that may surprise first-time visitors expecting Kyoto to have a more traditional-looking central train station. The station is large and bustling but not too difficult to navigate by following English signs. There are two information desks (marked with a "?" symbol) where you can ask for directions if lost.

Limousine buses from the airport arrive near the **Hachijo East entrance** at the southeast corner of the station and those arriving by the Shinkansen will find themselves on the south side of the station as well. There is a taxi stand outside this exit. You can take the **East Underground Walkway** directly to the northeast corner of the station, where you will find a municipal subway and bus information counter as well as ticket gates for the subway and another exit out of the station (the **JR Underground East exit**). You can also walk through the center of the station to the **JR Central exit** near which (on your left) you'll find the **Kyoto Tourist Information Center**. Most buses and taxis assemble outside the Central exit on the north side of the station.

Some hotels or inns will pick you up in a free shuttle bus at Kyoto Station or may have regularly scheduled hotel buses. When you book your accommodations, check for this service. You may need to reserve it beforehand. Check the details as the bus may depart from a station other than Kyoto Station, which you will have to reach by public transport.

Otherwise, taking a taxi is probably your best bet unless your accommodations are far from the station and you're concerned about costs. Even if drivers don't speak English, showing them the address, a map or the name of the hotel if it's a major one, will do the trick.

If you're staying quite far from Kyoto Station and don't want to run up a large taxi fare, you may want to take a municipal bus or the subway. Refer to the maps on pages 22–33 for bus routes around the city. There are a great many bus stops outside Kyoto Station, so if you're not sure which one to wait at ask at the information desk on the basement floor next to the subway entrances. The subway system is quite easy to navigate as it only has two lines. Refer to the plan of Kyoto Station on pages 10–11 of this book.

Kyoto Station

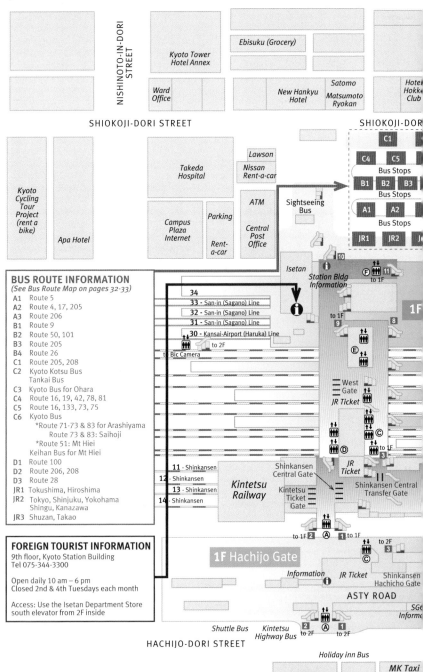

NISHINOTO-IN-DORI STREET

Kyoto Tower Hotel Annex

Ebisuku (Grocery)

Ward Office

New Hankyu Hotel

Satomo Matsumoto Ryokan

Hotel Hokke Club

SHIOKOJI-DORI STREET

SHIOKOJI-DOR

Kyoto Cycling Tour Project (rent a bike)

Apa Hotel

Takeda Hospital

Campus Plaza Internet

Parking

Rent-a-car

Lawson

Nissan Rent-a-car

ATM

Central Post Office

Sightseeing Bus

Isetan

Station Bldg Information

C1

C4 C5

Bus Stops

B1 B2 B3

Bus Stops

A1 A2

Bus Stops

JR1 JR2

10

to 1F 11

1F

to 1F 9

8

to 1F

West Gate
JR Ticket

BUS ROUTE INFORMATION
(See Bus Route Map on pages 32-33)
A1 Route 5
A2 Route 4, 17, 205
A3 Route 206
B1 Route 9
B2 Route 50, 101
B3 Route 205
B4 Route 26
C1 Route 205, 208
C2 Kyoto Kotsu Bus
    Tankai Bus
C3 Kyoto Bus for Ohara
C4 Route 16, 19, 42, 78, 81
C5 Route 16, 133, 73, 75
C6 Kyoto Bus
    *Route 71-73 & 83 for Arashiyama
     Route 73 & 83: Saihoji
    *Route 51: Mt Hiei
    Keihan Bus for Mt Hiei
D1 Route 100
D2 Route 206, 208
D3 Route 28
JR1 Tokushima, Hiroshima
JR2 Tokyo, Shinjuku, Yokohama
     Shingu, Kanazawa
JR3 Shuzan, Takao

34
33 - San-in (Sagano) Line
32 - San-in (Sagano) Line
31 - San-in (Sagano) Line
30 - Kansai-Airport (Haruka) Line
to 2F
Bic Camera

JR Ticket

FOREIGN TOURIST INFORMATION
9th floor, Kyoto Station Building
Tel 075-344-3300

Open daily 10 am – 6 pm
Closed 2nd & 4th Tuesdays each month

Access: Use the Isetan Department Store
south elevator from 2F inside

11 - Shinkansen
12 - Shinkansen
13 - Shinkansen
14 - Shinkansen

Kintetsu Railway

Kintetsu Ticket Gate

Shinkansen Central Gate

Shinkansen Central Transfer Gate

JR Ticket

to 1F 2 1 to 1F

to 2F 3

1F Hachijo Gate

Information

JR Ticket

Shinkansen Hachicho Gate

ASTY ROAD

SG
Informa

to 1F 2 A 1

Shuttle Bus

Kintetsu Highway Bus

to 2F A 1 to 2F

HACHIJO-DORI STREET

Holiday inn Bus

Nippon Rent-a-car

MK Taxi

Mazda Rent-a-car

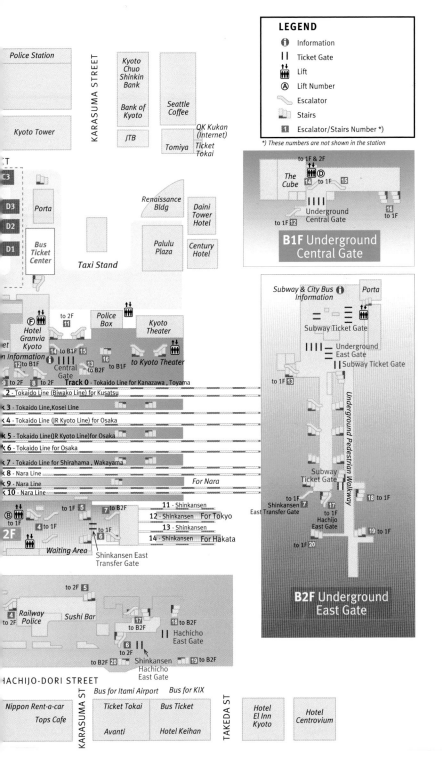

LEGEND

- ℹ️ Information
- ‖ Ticket Gate
- 🛗 Lift
- Ⓐ Lift Number
- Escalator
- Stairs
- **1** Escalator/Stairs Number *)

*) These numbers are not shown in the station

Police Station

KARASUMA STREET

Kyoto Chuo Shinkin Bank

Bank of Kyoto

JTB

Kyoto Tower

Seattle Coffee

QK Kukan (Internet)

Tomiya

Ticket Tokai

B1F Underground Central Gate

The Cube

to 1F & 2F

14 Ⓓ to 1F **15**

16 to 1F

Underground Central Gate

to 1F **12**

C3

D3

D2

D1

Porta

Bus Ticket Center

Taxi Stand

Renaissance Bldg

Daini Tower Hotel

Palulu Plaza

Century Hotel

Subway & City Bus Information ℹ️

Porta

Subway Ticket Gate

Underground East Gate
Subway Ticket Gate

Ⓕ 🛗
Hotel Granvia Kyoto

to 2F **11**

Police Box

Kyoto Theater

🛗

Information ℹ️

14 to B1F **15**

16

to 1F

to Kyoto Theater

Central Gate

12 to B1F

9 to 2F **8** to 2F **13** to B2F to 1F

Track 0 - Tokaido Line for Kanazawa , Toyama

2 - Tokaido Line (Biwako Line) for Kusatsu

3 - Tokaido Line, Kosei Line

4 - Tokaido Line (JR Kyoto Line) for Osaka

5 - Tokaido Line (JR Kyoto Line) for Osaka

6 - Tokaido Line for Osaka

7 - Tokaido Line for Shirahama , Wakayama

8 - Nara Line

9 - Nara Line   For Nara

10 - Nara Line

to 1F **13**

Underground Pedestrian Walkway

Subway Ticket Gate

to 1F **7**
Shinkansen East Transfer Gate

17 to 1F
Hachijo East Gate

18 to 1F

19 to 1F

to 1F **20**

Ⓑ 🛗
to 1F
4 to 1F

2F

🛗

Waiting Area

to 2F **5**

7 to B2F

6 to 1F

Shinkansen East Transfer Gate

11 - Shinkansen

12 - Shinkansen   For Tokyo

13 - Shinkansen

14 - Shinkansen   For Hakata

B2F Underground East Gate

to 2F **5**

4
to 2F
Railway Police

Sushi Bar

17 to B2F

18 to B2F
Hachijo East Gate

6 to 2F

to B2F **20**

Shinkansen Hachicho East Gate

19 to B2F

HACHIJO-DORI STREET

KARASUMA ST

Bus for Itami Airport   Bus for KIX

TAKEDA ST

Nippon Rent-a-car

Tops Cafe

Ticket Tokai

Avanti

Bus Ticket

Hotel Keihan

Hotel El Inn Kyoto

Hotel Centrovium

Kyoto Regional Train and Subway Network

Part 2: GETTING AROUND KYOTO

Kyoto's Transportation Network

Kyoto's municipal transportation system consists of two subway lines, one running roughly north–south (the green Karasuma Line) and the other roughly east–west (the vermilion Tozai Line), and an extensive network of buses. There is also the JR (Japan Rail) system and several private rail lines as well as a few tram, cable car and ropeway lines that make for a colorful journey. Taxis are also a convenient option and getting around by bicycle is quite practical as the city is largely flat and manageably sized.

The difference between public (city-run) trains and buses and those run by private companies need not concern the traveler or the average user. More or less the same procedures are used for all of them. It is important to keep in mind that both trains and buses stop running at a certain hour of the night (little public transportation runs after midnight) and that English signage may be limited. For example, the name of a station will be written in English on the platform but guide maps above the ticket machines may be in Japanese only. Plan a route in advance and keep this book with you for reference.

Riding the Bus

Much of Kyoto is not served by any subway or rail line and buses are a key mode of transport. You can get most anywhere by bus but rides can be long, and if you have to wait a long time for the bus and change buses one

Kyoto city bus

or more times, you may be worn out by the time you reach your destination. Try to identify the fastest route when there are multiple route choices (see maps, pages 22–33) and don't try to zip all over Kyoto in one day by bus. If visiting multiple tourist attractions in a day, it's best to choose ones that are reasonably close to one another and leave things on the far side of the city for another day.

Many **Kyoto city buses** are tinted green and all have their number and destination(s) displayed on a panel above the front windshield as well as next to the back door. Buses cost ¥220 within the city center. Outside the city center, fares increase depending on the distance traveled. Get on the bus at the back and take a ticket from the dispenser next to the door or insert a prepaid card (see **Rail Passes and Prepaid Cards**, page 16). This will be used to determine your fare if you go outside the ¥220 flat fare zone. There may be no ticket dispensers on some buses.

If you hear your destination announced, press a button next to the window to request a stop. Disembark from the front after putting the ticket and fare in the receptacle. If you don't have the exact change, use the change machine, then count out the amount you need. Do not put bills, ¥500 coins and so forth directly in the coin receptacle. If unsure, show your money and ticket to the driver and he will point to the proper slot. There is also a separate slot for prepaid cards.

The two major **private** rail line **operators** in Kyoto, **Hankyu and Keihan**, also operate buses that are used in the same manner as Kyoto city buses. Some prepaid cards such as the One-Day Pass cannot be used on these.

The city of Kyoto operates three **Raku Bus sightseeing buses** (*raku* being an old-time, uniquely Kyotoite word for "city" and also meaning "easy, simple" in Japanese). These buses take people from the Kyoto Station bus terminal to multiple tourist attractions on a single trip. They have on-board English announcements and are a convenient option for people with limited time to spend in Kyoto.

Kyoto Station

Bus 100 goes to the Kyoto National Museum and Sanjusangen-do Temple (Hakubutsukan-Sanjusangendo-mae stop), Kiyomizu-dera Temple (Kiyomizu-michi), Yasaka Shrine (Gion), Heian Shrine and Okazaki Park (Kyoto Kaikan-Bijutsukan-mae), Nanzenji and Eikan-do temples and The Philosopher's Walk (Miyanomae-cho), Ginkaku-ji Temple (Ginkakuji-mae) and Chion-in Temple (Jingu-michi). Bus 101 goes to Nijo Castle (Nijojo-mae), Seimei Shrine (Horikawa-Marutamachi), Nishijin Textile Center (Horikawa-Imadegawa), Kitano Tenmangu Shrine (Kitano-Tenmangu-mae), Kinkaku-ji Temple (Kinkakuji-michi) and Daitoku-ji Temple (Daitokuji-mae). Bus 102 goes from Ginkaku-ji Temple to Kinkaku-ji Temple via Daitoku-ji Temple (see map, pages 22–3).

Taking the Subway or Train

The **subway system** in Kyoto is not extensive but it is a quick way to travel north–south or east–west in central Kyoto. From Keage Station, for example, near Nanzen-ji and other temples on the east side, to Nijojo-mae Station (in front of Nijo Castle) west of central Kyoto takes under 10 minutes, the quickest means of making this trip by public transportation. Also, both subway lines connect directly to private rail lines reaching destinations outside Kyoto: the north–south Karasuma line connects to the Kintetsu Kyoto Line, reaching Nara in under an hour from Kyoto Station, and the east–west Tozai Line connects to the Keihan Keishin Line to Otsu and Lake Biwa.

The **Hankyu and Keihan railways** serve parts of Kyoto and can also be used to reach Kobe, Osaka and Otsu, and the Kintetsu Line goes to Nara. JR, Japan's nationwide railway, is primarily used for getting away from Kyoto rather than traveling within it. It can be used to reach points throughout Japan if your visit to Kyoto is part of a longer journey.

The challenges in riding trains and subways are threefold: buying tickets or prepaid cards from machines; making sure you are headed in the right direction; and going out of the correct exit when you arrive.

When buying a ticket, first of all be sure that you're using the right machine as some stations serve multiple train lines and tickets for each line are bought from separate banks of machines. Look for your destination on the route map above the machines, identify the route price and put that amount or more into the machine. Newer machines have a touch screen mechanism while older ones have physical buttons, but both will light up with numerals showing the fares that you can choose from (if you put in a ¥500 coin, for example, 230, 270, 310, 360 and 420 might light up). Push the button for the correct amount and take your ticket and change.

Rechargeable, contactless prepaid card

If you are not sure of the amount, buy the lowest-priced ticket. You will be able to make up the difference at your destination. There are generally fare adjustment machines inside the ticket gates that allow you to pay the difference or you can show the ticket to a station attendant who will tell you how much to pay.

If you're planning to ride the train a few times, prepaid cards are the sensible option as you won't have to bother with buying a ticket each time you get on the train. See the section on **Rail Passes and Prepaid Cards** below for details.

Before getting on the train, make sure you're headed in the right direction by checking the final destination or the next station. At the stairs leading up or down to the platform there are signs indicating the final destination and sometimes other key stops along the way, and there are often signs on the wall facing the platform showing the name of the particular station and the stations behind and ahead of this one. Check the information gleaned from signs against the train and subway map on page 17.

Once you've gotten off the train, look for signboards indicating which exit to go out of. There are often yellow signs on platforms and more outside the ticket gates near the exits indicating which way to go or which exit to take for various major streets, facilities, tourist attractions and so forth. Also outside the ticket gates, at major stations, are maps of the station showing the exits and maps of the neighborhood. If the station is a large one, identifying which exit is closest to your destination and which way you should walk once you get out will save a lot of hassle as exits may be far removed from one another.

If transferring to another train line, follow the signs. It may be necessary to go out of the ticket gate once and then back through another set of ticket gates. In general, things are well signposted in English.

Rail Passes and Prepaid Cards

There are rail passes providing special deals only available to tourists who do not live in Japan, such as the one-, two- or three-week **Japan Rail Pass** (intended for long-distance rail travel and not useful for getting around Kyoto and environs), and the **Kansai Thru Pass** (also known as the **Surutto Kansai two-day** or **three-day ticket**), which is quite useful for people who are planning to do a lot of train or bus travel over two or three days. Note that these days do not have to be consecutive; they can be scattered throughout the term of validity, usually a couple of months.

While the Japan Rail Pass is not the way to get around Kyoto and the surrounding area, if you are planning to do a lot of train travel around Japan, you may want to purchase one. You will first buy an "Exchange Order" outside Japan, from JTB Corporation, Nippon Travel Agency, Kintetsu International, Toptour Corporation, Japan Airlines (JAL), All Nippon Airways (ANA), JALPAK or their associated agencies. (When purchasing from JAL or ANA, you must book one of their flights as well.) Visit www.japanrailpass.net/ for a list of offices of these agencies in your country. When you arrive in Japan, you must show your Exchange Order and passport to obtain the actual rail pass. Japan Rail Pass Exchange Offices are located at major airports (Narita, Haneda, Kansai, etc.) and major train stations, including Kyoto Station. See www.japanrailpass.net/ for a complete list as well as prices, etc. The Japan Rail Pass has Ordinary and Green versions, the Green one being more expensive and allowing you to sit in superior-class Green train cars.

To get around Kyoto and vicinity, there is the **Kansai Thru Pass**. A two-day pass costs ¥3,800 and a three-day ¥5,000, which buys unlimited travel in the Kansai region on all *non-JR trains* (an important point to remember), all municipal buses (Kyoto, Kobe, Osaka) and most other bus lines (excluding airport limousine buses) and cable cars, etc., plus discounted admission to many tourist attractions. It can be purchased at Kansai International Airport at the KAA Travel Desk between the north and south exits in the first floor International Arrivals Lobby, or at the Kyoto Station Bus Information Center at the Karasuma Gate of Kyoto Station. On the Kintetsu Line connecting Kyoto and Nara, an extra charge is required for rapid express trains when using the Kansai Thru Pass.

Kyoto's Railway and Subway Network

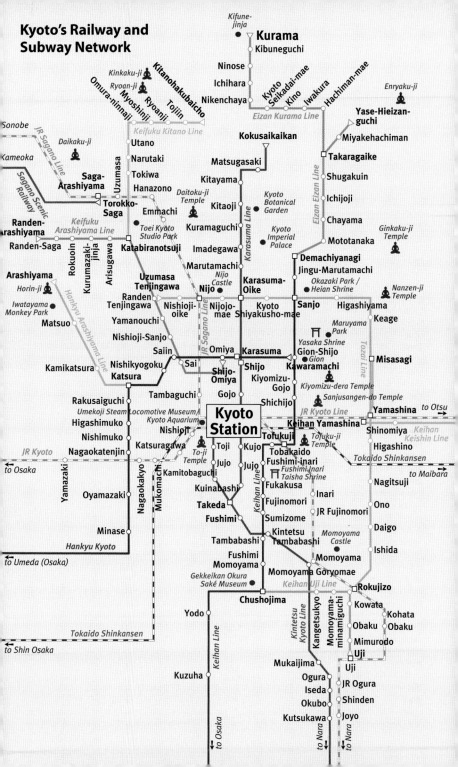

It may be possible to buy a Kansai Thru Pass outside of Japan before traveling. Consult your travel agent about this.

The **Kyoto Sightseeing One- and Two-day Pass Card** is cheaper than the Kansai Thru Pass but is only good on Kyoto city subways (the Karasuma and Tozai lines) and city buses inside a designated area. It costs ¥1,200 for one day and ¥2,000 for two. There is also a ¥500 one-day unlimited city bus pass, the **City Bus All-day Pass Card**, which is a good deal if you are going to ride city buses three or more times on a given day. These passes do not have to be used the day you buy them. You can buy them in advance and use them when needed. The Kyoto Sightseeing One- and Two-day Pass Card is available from ticket machines, and the City Bus All-day Pass from bus and subway information offices, windows next to ticket gates (when staffed) and on most buses.

Prepaid magnetic cards can be bought from the same banks of machines as train tickets, though some machines may not dispense them. They are inserted into the ticket gate and removed, just like a ticket, and the balance is printed on the back. They allow you to take multiple rides without buying a new ticket every time and can be used on trains and buses. (Some cards may not be accepted in some places but the Surutto Kansai card is usable on the majority of trains and buses.)

A standard **Surutto Kansai** pass is a prepaid card in denominations of one, two, three or five thousand yen. It is valid for the same rail and bus lines as the Kansai Thru Pass, i.e. all train lines except JR and most bus lines. The card can also be used to buy tickets (for other people in your party, for example) from machines. Note that Surutto Kansai is sold throughout the Kansai region and is known by different names on different train lines. On Kyoto subways it is called the **Miyako Card**.

A **Traffica Kyoto Card** is less versatile than a Surutto Kansai pass, only being valid on Kyoto city subways and buses. It offers a 10% discount, however; in other words, a card costing ¥1,000 gives ¥1,100 worth of rides and a card costing ¥3,000 gives ¥3,300 worth.

Be aware that none of these prepaid cards will pay you back the balance left over if you don't use their entire value.

Perhaps the most convenient card if you are planning to take at least 8–10 train rides is the **ICOCA Card**, a rechargeable contactless smart card developed by Japan Railways but usable on nearly all trains in the Kyoto region and some buses (as of this writing, Kyoto municipal buses [the green ones] are scheduled to start accepting ICOCA some time in fiscal 2014 but have not started yet). It can also be used interchangeably with similar contactless cards sold elsewhere in Japan, such as Tokyo's SUICA Card. It costs ¥2,000, of which ¥500 is a deposit, meaning that it will have ¥1,500 on it at first. ICOCA can be purchased and recharged by adding more yen to it at some, but not all, ticket vending machines. Look for the logo or the system's friendly mascot, a blue platypus named Ico-chan.

The ICOCA Card does not need to be inserted but only passed over the card reader at the ticket gate, so many people leave it in their wallets when they pass it over. (Keep in mind that if there are other contactless cards in your wallet, such as the SUICA Card, it will confuse the card reader and you won't be allowed through.) When you pass through the ticket gate, the balance on your card will be shown.

Before leaving Japan, you can return the card to a station attendant and get back your ¥500 deposit plus any remaining balance. (A ¥210 processing fee is deducted from this so, for example, if there were ¥400 left on your card, you would get ¥690 back rather than ¥900.)

With all of these confusing options, many travelers may be liable to give up on buying passes or prepaid cards and just stick with tickets. Cards are a lot more convenient, however, and can save money if you know which one to purchase. A handy summary to help you choose the right card is given below:

Japan Rail Pass

Purchase when: You will be traveling around Japan on Shinkansen (bullet trains) or other JR intercity trains. For example, if you are simply traveling from Tokyo to Kyoto and back again by Shinkansen, you will not save money by buying a Japan Rail Pass, but if you are traveling from Tokyo to Kyoto, on to Hiroshima or Kyushu, and *then* back to Tokyo in a single week, you will save a considerable amount.

Kansai Thru Pass

Purchase when: You will have two or three days during your stay in Kyoto that involve a fair amount of riding trains, subways and/or buses, and some of these may be private rail lines or buses (Hankyu, Keihan, Kintetsu, etc.) rather than municipal transport, or your destination is some distance from the city center.

Kyoto Sightseeing One- /Two-day Pass Card
Purchase when: You will have one or two days during your stay in Kyoto that involve a fair amount of riding non-JR trains or buses, and you're sure these are municipal subways or Kyoto city buses (all the numbered routes are city buses).

Kyoto Tourist One-day Pass

City Bus All-day Pass Card
Purchase when: You will ride Kyoto city buses three or more times on a given day and you're not going far from the city center. Arashiyama, Sagano and day-trip destinations such as Takao in the section on **Sidetrips Around Kyoto**, for example, are not covered by this pass.

Surutto Kansai Card
Purchase when: You will be riding buses, subways and/or non-JR trains multiple times and you aren't sure if these belong to the Kyoto municipal system or not, or you are planning to take side trips around Kyoto.

Traffica Kyoto Card
Purchase when: You will be riding Kyoto city subways and buses multiple times but not necessarily in the same one- or two-day period.

ICOCA Card
Purchase when: You'll be riding trains (possibly buses as well, as Kyoto city buses are scheduled to start accepting them sometime between April 2014 and March 2015) at least 8-10 times. These are the quickest and easiest to use on trains. The ICOCA can be used in Tokyo as well if you will be spending time there.

Taxis
Taxis in Kyoto are plentiful and can deliver you right to where you're going rather than to a train station or bus stop that may be some distance away. While they may be a bit more expensive than taxis in other developed nations (around ¥65 for the first two kilometers and about ¥100 for each several hundred meters thereafter), if there is a group of 3–4 people, taxis can be just as affordable as taking the bus or train and much less of a hassle. Indeed, it may well be the best option if you are a group of several people going a reasonably short distance. Note that four is the maximum number of passengers per vehicle (excluding the driver).

Taxis display electronic signs in kanji characters on the lower corner of the windshield that indicate their status as "occupied" (a green sign) or "available" (a red sign). Be aware that the taxi driver remotely opens and closes the left rear door so you do not need to open or shut it yourself.

Many taxis accept credit cards but not all. Look on the inside of the rear door for stickers showing the credit cards accepted. In general, Japan is a cash-based society and it should not be taken for granted that every shop, restaurant, etc. accepts credit cards either. The vast majority of taxis are non-smoking but some operated by individuals or smaller companies not belonging to the Kyoto Taxi Association may not be. Again, look for stickers on the windows. Stricter smoking regulations have been catching on little by little in Japan though smoking is still allowed in places, such as many cafés and restaurants, where it has been banned in most Western countries.

Most taxi drivers speak little or no English, but even if you have trouble communicating

Kyoto taxi

your destination, you can always write it down or show it to the driver on a map. The fare is shown on the meter and prices are not negotiable. Tips are not required or expected, though they might well be appreciated.

Another advantage is that taxis also run all night whereas public transportation shuts down around midnight.

Sightseeing Taxis

MK Taxi and Yasaka Taxi, the same two companies that run competing jumbo taxi airport shuttle services (see page 7) also operate chartered sightseeing taxi services with drivers who speak English, and in the case of MK Taxi, French, Korean and Spanish as well. Tours may last anywhere from two to nine hours and fees are charged by the hour, generally between ¥5,000 and ¥10,000 per hour, which is not too bad if several people are sharing. You can request a customized tour of the sights you want to see. This could be a good option, particularly if there are elderly or physically disabled people in your party.

Yasaka Taxi's website also states that they can make arrangements for dinner, theater tickets or entertainment by *maiko* (apprentice geisha) "at no extra charge," though the entertainment itself may be quite pricey even if the arrangements are free. See www.yasaka.jp/english/ or www.mk-group.co.jp/english/sightseeing/.

Renting a Bicycle

If you are fond of cycling, renting a bicycle is an inexpensive, healthy and environmentally friendly option. Built in a low-lying basin, Kyoto is largely flat. There is a bike path along the Kamo River that makes a quick, scenic and safe north–south route. The mountains in the distance make it easy to navigate. Only the south side of the city has no mountains,

Nothing is more pleasant than a riverside bicycle ride on a spring day.

so one's mental compass can be aligned at a glance. Cycling can also take you down back streets too narrow for a car to navigate. It's an ideal way to discover the mysterious and offbeat charms of the city. Be sure to ride carefully, safely and at a moderate speed as some parts of Kyoto are full of narrow lanes with poor visibility.

Kyoto Cycling Tour Project (KCTP) operates four cycling terminals in the city where bicycles can be rented for between ¥1,000 for a standard-class three-speed city bike and ¥2,000 for a special-class mountain bike per day. The bicycle can be returned at any one of the four terminals, though this terminal must be decided in advance. The terminals are located near Kyoto Station, near Kinkaku-ji Temple, in Nishiki-kita near Shijo and in Fushimi in the south part of the city (see maps, pages 21, 22–3).

There's also Tabi Chari, with four locations: in Higashiyama (at the Westin Miyako Hotel), Arashiyama (at the Restaurant Arashiyama), Central Kyoto (at the Kyoto Tokyu Hotel) and North Kyoto (at the Grand Prince Hotel in Takaragaike) (see maps, pages 21, 22–3). They rent electric-assisted bicycles for ¥2,000 per day as does Kyo no Raku Chari on Higashi Oji street near the Higashiyama subway station. These bicycles give you a magical zip and make it a breeze to get up hills. Carillon, with locations in Demachiyanagi and Kitaoji, rents standard-issue one-speed bicycles for just ¥500 per day with the option to extend until next morning for ¥250.

The city of Kyoto has also launched a public Community Cycle program which rents bicycles by the hour, with five terminals: at Keihan Sanjo Station behind the shopping mall at Sanjo-Kawabata, at Kyoto Yodobashi Station on the 2nd floor of the Yodobashi Camera store, at Karasuma-Oike Station north of the Manga Museum, at Jingu Marutamachi Station on Kawabata-dori south of Maruta-machi Station (2nd floor) and at Shichijo-Nishi Station on Kawabata-dori at the southwest corner of Shichijo-Kawabata. You must pay with a credit card. Bikes may be returned at any of the five stations.

Kyoto Cycling Tour Project offers various half-day or full-day cycling tours of Kyoto with an English-speaking guide (the Backstreet Tour, the Machiya [townhouse] Tour, the Mystery Tour, etc.), which are quite popular. See their website www.kctp.net/en/ for details.

Kyoto Bicycle Rental Shops

2 km
1 mile

N

Mt. Momoyama
460m

OMIYA
TRAFFIC PARK

Daitoku-ji

Kinkaku-ji

Tabi Chari

Kokusaikaikan

TAKARAGAIKE
PARK

Takaraga-ike

Kita-Oji-dori

Shimogamo Hon-dori

Shimogamo-jinja

Yuhukae-no-michi

na-ji

KCTP
Tel: 075 354 3636
Kitanohakubaicho

Nishioji-dori

Imadegawa-dori

Carillon
Tel: 075 200 8219

Kyoto Imperial
Palace ★

Kawaramachi-dori

Placemark 3
Station

Imadegawa-dori

YOSHIDAYAMA
PARK

Higashi Oji-dori

Daiko
Tel: 075 431 4522

Marutamachi-dori

Sagano Line

Nijo

Nijo Castle ★

Karasuma Oike
Minaport Station

Marutamachi-dori

Jingu Marutamachi
Minaport Station

Kyo no Raku Chari
Tel: 075 761 5828/
050 1300 1653
Free: 0120 318 319

Randentenjingawa

Horikawa-dori

Karasuma-oike

Oike-dori

Kyotoshiyakushomae

Sanjo-dori

Keage

Sanjo Minaport
Station

Tabi Chari

Cycle Dream
075 323-3666

Sai

Omiya

KCTP
Tel: 075 354 3636

Karasuma

Shijo

Kawaramachi

J Cycle
Tel: 075 341 3196

Gojo-dori

Gojo Cycle
Tel: 075 746 4855

Nishi
Hongan-ji

Gojo

Miyabiya
Tel: 075 354 7060

Gojo-dori

Kiyomizu-dera

Shichijo-dori

Fune Rental
Tel: 075 371 7800

Horikawa-dori

Yodobashi Camera
Station

Shichijo Nishi
Minaport Station

Kyoto

KCTP
Tel: 075 354 3636

Kyoto Station East
Rent a Cycle
Tel: 0120 318 319

Higashiyama Tunnel

Nishioji

Kyoto Eco Trip
Tel: 075 691 0794

Kawaramachi-dori

Tofukuji

Tofuku-ji

Sennyu-ji

Kujo-dori

Toba-kaido

Hanshin E'way

KCTP
Tel: 075 354 3636

Fushimi Inari
Taisha Shrine

Kuinabashi

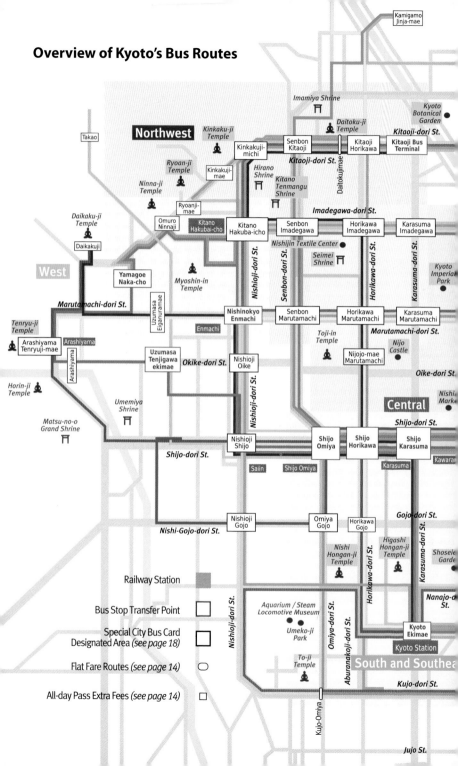

Overview of Kyoto's Bus Routes

Kamigamo
Jinja-mae

Imamiya Shrine

Kyoto
Botanical
Garden

Northwest

Kinkaku-ji Temple

Daitoku-ji Temple

Kitaoji-dori St.

Kinkakuji-michi

Senbon Kitaoji

Kitaoji Horikawa

Kitaoji Bus Terminal

Kitaoji-dori St.

Ryoan-ji Temple

Kinkakuji-mae

Hirano Shrine

Kitano Tenmangu Shrine

Daitokujimae

Ninna-ji Temple

Imadegawa-dori St.

Ryoanji-mae

Kitano Hakubai-cho

Kitano Hakuba-icho

Senbon Imadegawa

Horikawa Imadegawa

Karasuma Imadegawa

Daikaku-ji Temple

Omuro Ninnaji

Nishijin Textile Center

Karasuma-dori St.

Daikakuji

West

Seimei Shrine

Kyoto Imperial Park

Yamagoe Naka-cho

Myoshin-in Temple

Nishioji-dori St.

Senbon-dori St.

Horikawa-dori St.

Marutamachi-dori St.

Uzumasa Eiganuramae

Nishinokyo Enmachi

Senbon Marutamachi

Horikawa Marutamachi

Karasuma Marutamachi

Tenryu-ji Temple

Arashiyama

Arashiyama Tenryuji-mae

Arashiyama

Uzumasa Tenjigawa ekimae

Okike-dori St.

Enmachi

Nishioji Oike

Toji-in Temple

Nijojo-mae Marutamachi

Nijo Castle

Marutamachi-dori St.

Oike-dori St.

Horin-ji Temple

Umemiya Shrine

Nishioji-dori St.

Nishi Marke

Central

Matsu-no-o Grand Shrine

Shijo-dori St.

Nishioji Shijo

Shijo Omiya

Shijo Horikawa

Shijo Karasuma

Shijo-dori St.

Saiin

Shijo Omiya

Karasuma

Kawara

Nishioji Gojo

Omiya Gojo

Horikawa Gojo

Gojo-dori St.

Nishi-Gojo-dori St.

Nishi Hongan-ji Temple

Higashi Hongan-ji Temple

Karasuma-dori St.

Shoseie Garde

Nanajo-a St.

Railway Station

Bus Stop Transfer Point

Nishioji St.

Aquarium / Steam Locomotive Museum

Omiya-dori St.

Horikawa-dori St.

Kyoto Ekimae

Special City Bus Card Designated Area *(see page 18)*

Umeko-ji Park

Aburanokoji-dori St.

Kyoto Station

Flat Fare Routes *(see page 14)*

To-ji Temple

South and Southea

All-day Pass Extra Fees *(see page 14)*

Kujo-Omiya

Kujo-dori St.

Jujo St.

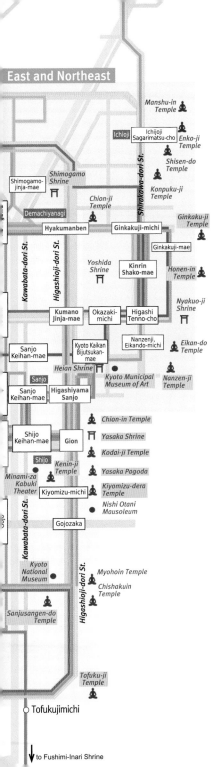

East and Northeast

There is a bewildering number of bus lines in Kyoto but a few are particularly useful for getting to major sightseeing destinations. **Buses 100, 101 and 102** are Easy Sightseeing Buses (Raku buses) intended for tourists, and between them cover many of the main attractions at a flat fare of ¥220. **Buses 100 and 101** depart from the bus stops to your right as you come out the central exit of Kyoto Station. **Bus 100** heads from Kyoto Station to the northeast corner of the city, stopping at Kyoto National Museum and Sanjusangen-do Temple (Hakubutsukan-Sanjusangendo-mae stop), Kiyomizu-dera Temple (Kiyomizu-michi), Yasaka Shrine (Gion), Heian Shrine and Okazaki Park (Kyoto Kaikan-Bijutsukan-mae), Nanzen-ji and Eikan-do temples and The Philosopher's Walk (Miyanomae-cho), Ginkaku-ji Temple (Ginkakuji-mae) and Chion-in Temple (Jingu-michi). **Bus 101** goes to the northwest, taking you to Nijo Castle (Nijojo-mae), Seimei Shrine (Horikawa-Marutamachi), Nishijin Textile Center (Horikawa-Imadegawa), Kitano Tenmangu Shrine (Kitano-Tenmangu-mae), Kinkaku-ji Temple (Kinkakuji-michi) and Daitoku-ji Temple (Daitokuji-mae).

Bus 102 serves northern Kyoto, from Ginkaku-ji Temple (Ginkakuji-michi) in the northeast across to Daitoku-ji Temple in the northwest. Most of the attractions it covers are also served by the **100** or **101** and it is primarily useful for getting across from east to west on the north side of Kyoto.

Buses 200–208 are a replacement for the old Kyoto streetcar network, sadly no longer running. They circulate around the main streets and can be useful for getting from one part of the city to another as well as hitting some of the major sights. **Bus 201** goes to Gion, **202** to Tofuku-ji Temple, **203** to Gion and Ginkaku-ji Temple, **204** to Kinkaku-ji Temple, **205** to Shimogamo Shrine and Kinkaku-ji Temple, **206** to Gion and Kinkaku-ji Temple and **207** and **208** to Tofuku-ji Temple.

Bus 5, also departing from Kyoto Station, stops at Heian Shrine and Okazaki Park, Nanzen-ji and Eikan-do temples, and Ginkaku-ji Temple. It largely follows the same route as **bus 100** and they can be used interchangeably.

To get from central Kyoto to western Kyoto, including Arashiyama, take **Bus 11** from Kawaramachi Sanjo or **Bus 28** from Kyoto Station. To get to Fushimi-Inari Taisha Shrine in the south, take **South 5** from Kyoto Station.

Central Kyoto Bus Stops and Routes

Kitano ←

Kitaoji ↑

12
9

Horikawa
Kamidachiuri

Imadegawa
Jofukuji

Imadegawa
Omiya

Kamigyoku
Sogochoshamae

Dochishamae

59
203 203
101

**HORIKAWA
IMADEGAWA**

**KARASUMA
IMADEGAWA**

IMADEGAWA-DORI ST.

IMADEGAWA-DORI .

Nishijin Textile Center ●

Seimei Shrine ⛩

Chijo
Modoribashi

Chiekoin
Nakadachiuri

Omiya
Nakadachiuri

HORIKAWA-DORI ST.

KARASUMA-DORI ST.

12
9

1 1

50

Horikawa
Nakadachiuri

50

Horikawa
Shimochojamachi

● *Kyoto Prefectural
Government Offices*

Horikawa
Shimodachiuri

Arashiyama ←

Marutamachi
Chiekoin

204

10
202 93

**HORIKAWA
MARUTAMACHI**

**KARASUMA
MARUTAMACHI**

10
202

MARUTAMACHI-DORI ST.

Fuchomae

MARUTAMACHI-DORI

□ All-day Pass Extra Fees *(see page 14)*

○ Flat Fare Routes *(see page 14)*

**NIJOJO-MAE
MARUTAMACHI**

*Kyoto International
Manga Museum*
●

Railway Station

Special City Bus Card
Designated Area *(see page 18)*

Bus Stop Transfer Point

HORIKAWA-DORI ST.

50

1 1

KARASUMA-DORI ST.

Horikawa Oike

9

12

Horikawa Sanjo

*Kyoto Natio
Museum*
●

Horikawa
Takoyakushi

↓ Shijo/ Kyoto Station

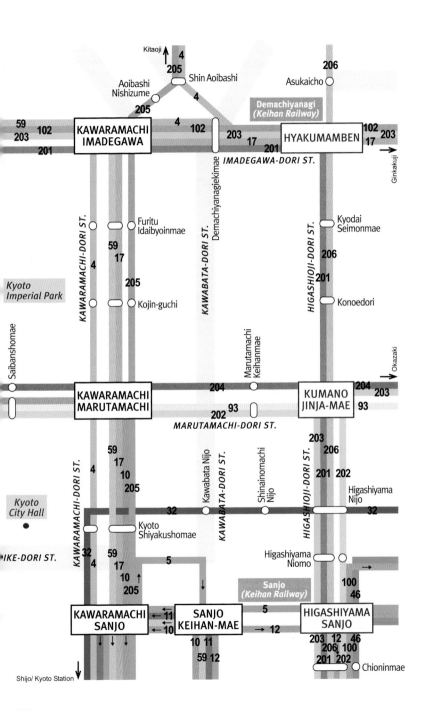

East and Northeast Kyoto Bus Stops and Routes

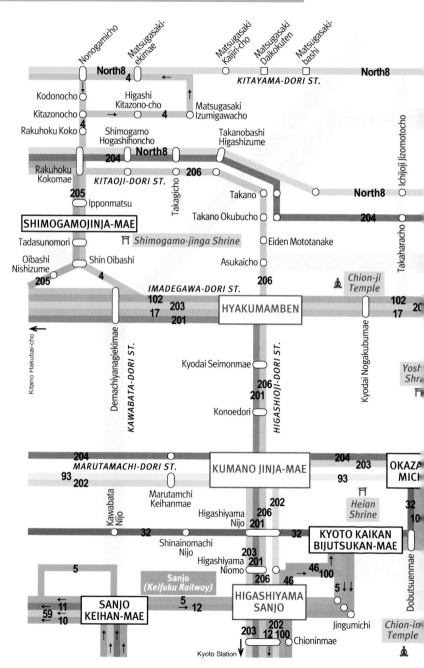

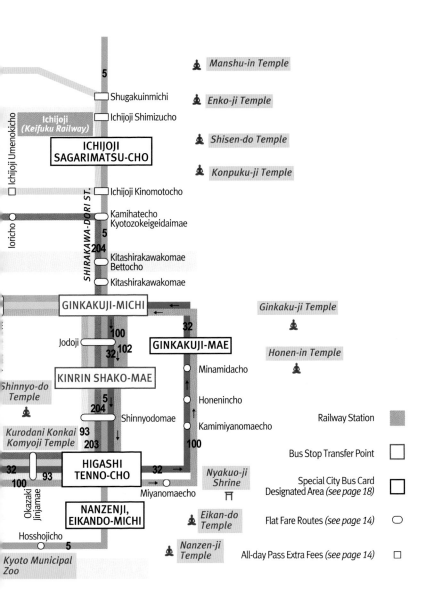

- **5** Shugakuinmichi
- Ichijoji Shimizucho
- **Manshu-in Temple**
- **Enko-ji Temple**

Ichijoji (Keifuku Railway)

Ichijoji Umenokicho

ICHIJOJI SAGARIMATSU-CHO

- **Shisen-do Temple**
- **Konpuku-ji Temple**

SHIRAKAWA-DORI ST.

- Ichijoji Kinomotocho
- Kamihatecho Kyotozokeigeidaimae
- **5 204**
- Kitashirakawakomae Bettocho
- Kitashirakawakomae

Ioricho

GINKAKUJI-MICHI

Ginkaku-ji Temple

Jodoji **100**
32 **32 102**
GINKAKUJI-MAE

Honen-in Temple

KINRIN SHAKO-MAE

- Minamidacho

Shinnyo-do Temple

- **5**
- **204**
- Shinnyodomae

- Honenincho
- Kamimiyanomaecho

Kurodani Konkai Komyoji Temple **93 203**

100

32 93

HIGASHI TENNO-CHO **32**

100

Okazaki Jinjamae

NANZENJI, EIKANDO-MICHI

- Miyanomaecho

Hosshojicho **5**

Kyoto Municipal Zoo

Nyakuo-ji Shrine

Eikan-do Temple

Nanzen-ji Temple

Railway Station	▣
Bus Stop Transfer Point	▢
Special City Bus Card Designated Area *(see page 18)*	▢
Flat Fare Routes *(see page 14)*	◯
All-day Pass Extra Fees *(see page 14)*	▢

Northwest Kyoto Bus Stops and Routes

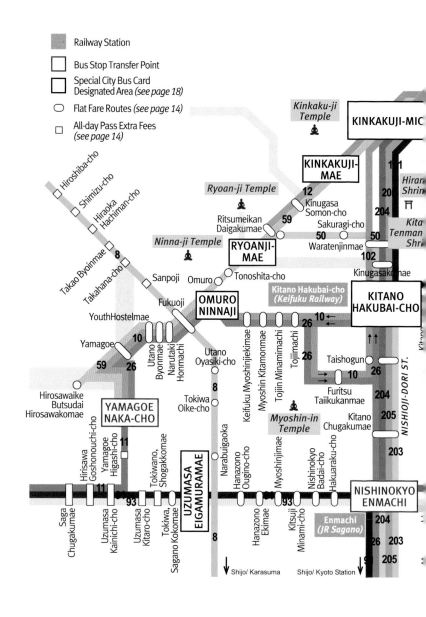

Legend:
- Railway Station
- Bus Stop Transfer Point
- Special City Bus Card Designated Area (see page 18)
- Flat Fare Routes (see page 14)
- All-day Pass Extra Fees (see page 14)

Kinkaku-ji Temple

KINKAKUJI-MIC

KINKAKUJI-MAE

Hiran Shrin

Hiroshiba-cho

Shimizu-cho

Hiraoka Hachiman-cho

Ryoan-ji Temple

12

20

204

Kinugasa Somon-cho

Kita Tenman Shri

Ritsumeikan Daigakumae

59

Sakuragi-cho

50

50

Takao Byoinmae

8

Ninna-ji Temple

RYOANJI-MAE

Waratenjinmae

102

Takahana-cho

Sanpoji

Omuro

Tonoshita-cho

Kinugasako mae

Fukuoji

OMURO NINNAJI

Kitano Hakubai-cho (Keifuku Railway)

KITANO HAKUBAI-CHO

YouthHostelmae

10

26

Yamagoe

10

26

Utano Byonmae

Narutaki Honmachi

Utano Oyasiki-cho

Keifuku Myoshinjiekimae

Myoshin Kitamonmae

Tojiin Minamimachi

Tojiimachi

26

Taishogun

26

59

26

10

Hirosawaike Butsudai Hirosawakomae

8

Tokiwa Oike-cho

Furitsu Taiikukanmae

204

YAMAGOE NAKA-CHO

Myoshin-in Temple

Kitano Chugakumae

205

Hirisawa Goshonouchi-cho

Yamagoe Higashi-cho

11

Tokiwano, Shogakkomae

Narabuigaoka

Hanazono Ougino-cho

Myoshinjimae

Nishinokyo Badai-cho

Hakuaraku-cho

203

11

UZUMASA EIGAMURAEMAE

NISHINOKYO ENMACHI

Saga Chugakumae

Uzumasa Kainichi-cho

Uzumasa Kitaro-cho

Tokiwa, Sagano Kokomae

93

Hanazono Ekimae

Kitsuji Minami-cho

93

Enmachi (JR Sagano)

204

8

Shijo/ Karasuma

Shijo/ Kyoto Station

26

203

205

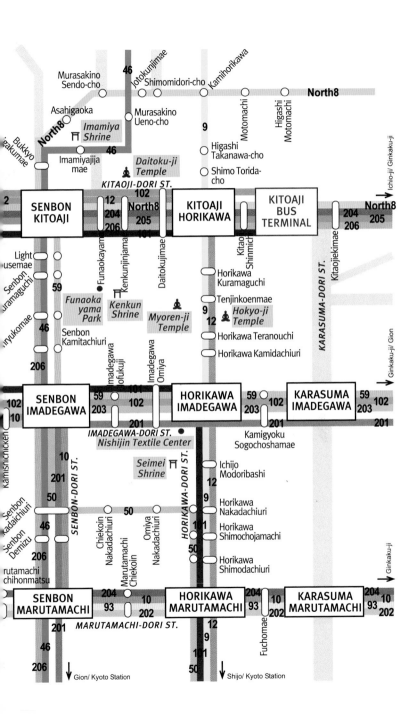

West Kyoto Bus Stops and Routes

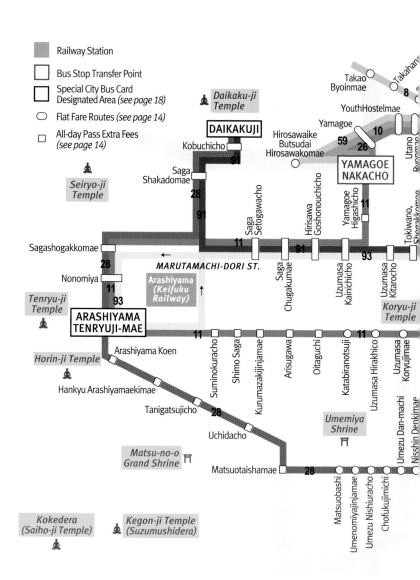

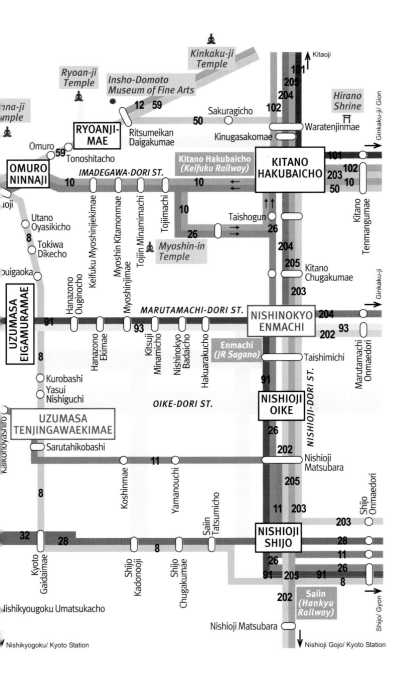

South and Southeast Kyoto Bus Stops and Routes

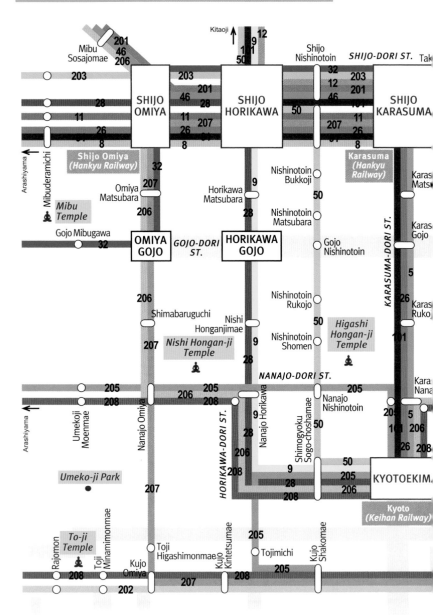

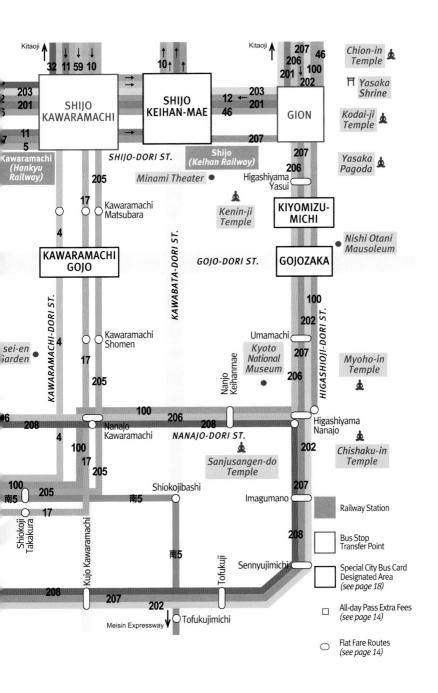

Part 3: MAPS OF KYOTO

Introducing Kyoto's Main Districts

Kyoto contains several districts in which sights are clustered close enough to enjoy exploring on foot, by bicycle or by short bus and taxi rides. This section of the book suggests where to go and how to get around each of Kyoto's main districts. Profiles of each district correspond with the Kyoto area maps on pages 44–71.

Map 1 KYOTO STATION AREA
- Kyoto Station 京都駅
- Kyoto Tower 京都タワー
- Nishi-Hongan-ji Temple 西本願寺
- Higashi Hongan-ji Temple 東本願寺
- Shosei-en Garden 渉成園
- Sanjusangen-do Temple Hall 三十三間堂
- Kyoto National Museum 京都国立博物館

Kyoto Station, a futuristic block of steel and glass that opened in 1997 to some controversy, is the main transportation hub of Kyoto City. This is the point where most visitors enter and leave the city and it's easy to zip off to other parts of the Kansai region and all over Japan from here. For this reason, there are quite a few major hotels in the vicinity of the station but not a whole lot to see. However, there are several major tourist attractions in the southern part of the city.

Outside the central (north) exit of Kyoto Station are a large number of buses and taxis. Beyond these you will see **Kyoto Tower**, a 131 m (426 ft) orange and white spire which, like the station building, may come as a modernist shock to those expecting a quainter and more traditional cityscape. The tower was built amid the forward-looking fervor surrounding the 1964 Tokyo Olympics and is regarded as a colossal blunder by some. Unlike most cities in Japan, Kyoto has a fair number of regulations governing building height, color, rooftop signage, neon and so forth, which help ensure that Kyoto Tower is by far the tallest and also one of the most garish structures in the city. At a height of 100 m (328 ft) is an observation platform (9 am–9 pm, ¥770) with 360-degree panoramic views. In the basement (B3 floor)

is a **public bath** (7 am–10.30 pm, ¥750, ¥450 kids). Public baths (*sento*), unlike natural hot springs (*onsen*), usually do not employ natural hot spring water but rather ordinary heated water, but they are generally found in convenient locations in urban neighborhoods and are an inexpensive and highly refreshing way to get off your feet and relax for a while.

Just a few minutes' walk north of Kyoto Station are **Nishi-Hongan-ji** and **Higashi Hongan-ji**, a pair of huge and historic temples still in use for religious purposes today, containing several impressive pieces of classic architecture as well as gardens. A short walk east of Higashi-Hongan-ji is **Shosei-en**, a detached annex of the temple with a contemplative pond and gardens. All are free to enter and provide respite from the bustle of downtown Kyoto. They also open very early in the morning (around 5–5.30 am, varying somewhat by season. Shosei-en only, 9 am–4.30 pm, free).

Between Kyoto Station and Kyoto Tower is Shiokoji-dori, a large east–west street. About 1 km (0.60 miles), or 20 minutes' walk, due east on Shiokoji-dori is **Sanjusangen-do**, a 13th-century Buddhist temple hall renowned for its 1,001 statues of the thousand-armed Kannon. There is one large statue, the main object of worship at the temple, and 1,000 more life-sized statues arrayed like a standing army, which is truly awe-inspiring. Sanjusangen-do literally means "hall of 33 intervals between columns," the number of spaces between columns being indicative of the length of the building. At 120 m (394 ft), it is Japan's longest wooden building. People with an interest in Buddhism or Buddhist art will certainly appreciate it. Walk or take Bus 101, 206 or 208 from Kyoto Station (Hakubutsukan-Sanjusangendo-mae bus stop). It's also a five minute walk from Shichijo Station on the Keihan Line (8 am–5 pm [9 am–4 pm, November 16–March 31], ¥600).

North of Sanjusangen-do, across the large east–west boulevard Shichijo-dori, is the

Kyoto National Museum, a grand Western-looking brick edifice with extensive collections of pre-modern art, antiques and artifacts from Japan and other Asian countries. Along with the Tokyo National Museum and Nara National Museum, it was originally an Imperial museum built to house the nation's treasures, and contains a great number of precious items on loan from temples, shrines and the Imperial Household itself. The museum will be closed on and off until end 2014 for renovations: check their website (www.kyohaku.go.jp) for up-to-date information. It's a five or ten minute walk from Shichijo Station on the Keihan Line or a one minute walk from Hakubutsukan Sanjusangendo-mae bus stop (Bus 206 or 208 from Kyoto Station) (9.30 am–6 pm Tuesday–Sunday, open until 8 pm Friday, closed Monday. Entrance fees vary depending on exhibition).

Map 2 KAWARAMACHI SHOPPING DISTRICT

■ Nishiki Market 錦市場
■ Kyoto International Manga Museum
　京都国際マンガミュージアム

One block north of Shijo-dori, which runs parallel to the Hankyu Kyoto Line, is the **Nishiki Market**, a lively shopping arcade full of all manner of local and traditional foods which is worth a visit even if for the

Nishiki Market

taste of old-time Kyoto commerce. Wonder at the number of types of pickles, among other things (generally 9 am–6 pm or so, free).

Central Kyoto has several unique museums devoted to traditional and not so traditional arts. *Manga* comics buffs should visit the **Kyoto International Manga Museum**, with a collection of 300,000 comics from throughout the medium's history housed in an old elementary school. There are special exhibitions, *kamishibai* (traditional storytelling with picture placards) performances that kids will enjoy, artists who will draw your *manga* portrait (on Fri., Sat. and Sun.) and more. Near Karasuma-Oike Station on the Karasuma or Tozai subway lines or Karasuma-Oike bus stop (10 am–6 pm, closed Wed., ¥800).

Map 3 GION AND KIYOMIZU AREA

■ Sanjo-dori 三条通
■ Kamo River 鴨川
■ Sanjo Ohashi Bridge 三条大橋
■ Kiyomizu-dera Temple 清水寺
■ Yasaka-no-to Pagoda (Hokan-ji Temple) 法観寺 八坂の塔
■ Kodai-ji Temple 高台寺
■ Maruyama Park 円山公園
■ Chion-in Temple 知恩院
■ Shoren-in Temple 青蓮院
■ Yasaka Shrine 八坂神社
■ Gion 祇園
■ Hanami-koji 花見小路
■ Kennin-ji Temple 建仁寺
■ Shijo-dori 四条通

Sanjo-dori, a large east–west street, more or less forms the north border of Gion and Higashiyama. It crosses the **Kamo River** at the **Sanjo Ohashi Bridge**, on the east side of which is the Sanjo-Keihan subway station and Sanjo Station on the Keihan Line. The Kamo riverbank is popular with walkers, joggers, cyclists, loungers, dog fanciers and local college kids. During the hot months (which last a long time, from May to September, and can be pretty sweltering) nearly a hundred **restaurants** along the western bank of the river offer outdoor terrace *kawayuka* dining on raised platforms where breezes blow from the river. The front entrances to the restaurants are on **Kiyamachi-dori**, a block west of the river, between Nijo and Gojo. Lunch is served in May and September only, dinner from May 1 to September 30. Prices vary and some restaurants may require reservations, but it's a quintessential Kyoto dining experience worth having.

Kiyomizu-dera Temple

Devote at least one day to perambulating the Higashiyama area alone as it's home to quite a few of Kyoto's best sights. Among these is **Kiyomizu-dera**, a sprawling hillside temple with splendid halls, pagodas and fall foliage. The temple has a large veranda 13 m (426 ft) above the hillside, offering splendid city views, from which the impetuous traditionally leapt in the hopes their wishes would be granted (a practice now forbidden) (6 am–6 pm, ¥300. During night-time illumination periods [mid-March to mid-April and mid-November to early December], also open 6.30 am–9.30 pm, ¥400. Gets crowded at these times.) The five-storied pagoda **Yasaka-no-to** of **Hokan-ji Temple**, one of Kyoto's most iconic landmarks, serenely dominates the view from Kiyomizu-dera. Also of great scenic beauty are the gardens of nearby **Kodai-ji Temple**, founded at the dawn of the Edo Period (around 1600) by Nene, the principal wife of daimyo Toyotomi Hideyoshi (9 am–5 pm, ¥600). She also gave her name to Nene-no-michi, the lovely and well-preserved stone-paved path leading from the foot of Sannen-zaka (the quaint if touristy street below Kiyomizu Temple) past Kodai-ji to **Maruyama Park**, a favorite spot for cherry blossom viewing. Branching off of Nene-no-michi to the west is the picturesque stone-flagged **Ishibei-koji alley**, an entertainment

quarter in days gone by and still home to traditional inns and exclusive Kyoto restaurants. Adjoining Maruyama Park to the north is the vast **Chion-in Temple**, known for its colossal Sanmon Gate and gardens (open 9 am–4 pm, gardens ¥500), and the tranquilly beautiful yet often overlooked **Shoren-in Temple** (9 am–4.30 pm, ¥500. Also open 6 pm–9.30 pm during night-time illumination [around November], ¥800). To the west is **Yasaka Shrine**, the main shrine of the Gion district.

Gion grew up around the shrine as a community serving the needs of shrine pilgrims and later evolved into Kyoto's most famous geisha district. Geisha, professional female entertainers and hostesses highly trained in traditional arts, are known in Kyoto as *geiko*, while young apprentice *geiko* are known as *maiko*. *Maiko* can sometimes be sighted outdoors in Gion, though there have been problems in recent years with mobbing by "maiko paparazzi" bent on taking photos of them. Do keep a respectful distance.

One of the most scenic parts of Gion is **Hanami-koji**, the main north–south pedestrian thoroughfare stretching 1 km (0.60 miles) from Sanjo-dori avenue past Shijo-dori and down to **Kennin-ji Temple**. It is lined with chic restaurants housed in preserved *machiya* townhouses, along with some genuine geisha teahouses, and much care is taken to preserve its historic atmosphere. Property taxes in the olden days were determined based on the width of a building's frontage, which led Kyoto townhouses to be constructed with an *unagi no nedoko* (eel's nest) layout, narrow but very deep. Gion is a good place to spot faithfully preserved examples of this traditional vernacular architecture. Also idyllic and considerably quieter is the area surrounding the willow-lined **Shirakawa Canal**, which runs more or less parallel to Sanjo-dori and Shijo-dori (i.e. east–west) between the two avenues.

Shijo-dori is one of Kyoto's busiest streets, with its eastern end at Yasaka Shrine. Cross the Kamo River on either the Shijo or Sanjo bridges and you'll enter downtown Kyoto, less picturesque but a better place to find affordable restaurants, have a cup of coffee or a drink, or purchase necessities. A couple of blocks west of the river and running parallel to it (north–south) is the smaller **Takase River**, once a commercial canal and today the heart of a dining and leisure district more accessible than those of Gion. Lined with cherry trees, it makes for a pleasant stroll.

Map 4 HEIAN SHRINE AREA

■ Okazaki Park 岡崎公園
■ Kyoto Municipal Museum of Art 京都市美術館
■ National Museum of Modern Art 京都国立近代美術館
■ Kyoto Municipal Zoo 京都市動物園
■ Heian Shrine 平安神宮
■ Nanzen-ji 南禅寺

Culture, nature and history are nestled in sedate surroundings in this area of Kyoto.

From the Kamo River (see Map 3, pages 48–9), about 20 minutes' walk to the east on Sanjo-dori, is **Okazaki Park**, with one of Japan's largest *torii* shrine gates at its

Heian Shrine

entrance. To the right of the gate is the **Kyoto Municipal Museum of Art** (9 am–5 pm, closed Mon., admission varies), exhibiting both old and new art primarily from Japan, and to the left is the **National Museum of Modern Art**, Kyoto, showing modern and contemporary art from both Japan and abroad (9.30 am–5 pm, till 8 pm on Fri., April through October, closed Mon., ¥420). Inside the park is the **Kyoto Municipal Zoo**, a compact zoo with all the usual suspects (9 am–4.30 pm, closed Mon., ¥600, kids free), and to the north of the park is **Heian Shrine**, an imposing shrine with extensive scenic gardens built about a hundred years ago as a replica of an ancient palace (6 am–5 pm, gardens ¥600). You can reach Okazaki Park by Bus 5, 32, 46 or 100 (Kyoto Kaikan Bijutsukan-mae stop).

Further east (toward the mountains) from the park is **Nanzen-ji**, headquarters of the Rinzai Zen sect and one of Kyoto's most impressive and beautiful temples (8.30 am–4 pm, ¥500). There are some quieter subtemples around the main temple. To the right of the main temple entrance you can see an incongruous red brick Western-looking aqueduct. Go around to the other side of it and follow the trail upward, and it connects to a hiking course to the top of Mt Daimonji. It takes an hour or less to reach the top, where you will be rewarded with a splendid view.

Map 5 KYOTO IMPERIAL PALACE

■ Kyoto Imperial Palace 京都御所
■ Kyoto Gyoen Park 京都御苑

At the heart of Kyoto is the **Kyoto Imperial Palace**, home to the Emperor for centuries until he moved to Tokyo in 1869. The buildings are preserved and free tours are offered. Apply in advance with your passport at the Imperial Household Agency (located near the northwest corner of the spacious **Kyoto Gyoen Park** surrounding the palace). The agency accepts same-day applications for tours in person, or apply well in advance (before coming to Japan) on its website: www.sankan.kunaicho.go.jp/english/. English tours are at 10 am and 2 pm Monday to Friday. Once you get permission, arrive at the meeting point 20 minutes before the tour time. It's also pleasant just to stroll through the park. Imadegawa Station (Karasuma subway line) or bus to Karasuma-Imadegawa (Park, always open, free).

Map 6 NIJO CASTLE AREA
■ Nijo Castle 二条城
■ Seimei Shrine 晴明神社
■ Raku Art Museum 楽美術館

During the Edo Period, the Tokugawa shoguns established a private Kyoto residence near the Imperial Palace at **Nijo Castle**, one of Kyoto's most important historic sites. A testament to the shogun's prosperity and might, it has lavish interiors, splendid screen paintings, marvelous gardens, hidden chambers and staircases and squeaking "nightingale floors" that alerted residents to intruders. Nijo Castle is about ten blocks southwest of the Imperial Palace Park. Nijojomae Subway (Tozai subway line) (entry 8.45 am–4 pm, gates close at 5 pm, ¥600).

Much smaller but also of historic interest is **Seimei Shrine**, enshrining Abe no Seimei, legendary mystic and oracle to the Emperor during the Heian Period about 1,000 years ago. He was a master of Onmyodo, an esoteric cosmology employing the principles of yin and yang. The shrine features many pentagrams, a symbol more familiar from Western occultism, including one on a well said to contain magical water. South of the shrine is **Ichijo-Modoribashi**, a mystical bridge. Renowned tea master Sen no Rikyu brewed tea using the shrine's well water, and had his head displayed on the bridge after his forced ritual suicide.

Meanwhile, the **Raku Art Museum** exhibits *raku* ware, the hand-shaped pottery often used in the tea ceremony. Located next to the home and workshop of the Raku family, now in its 15th generation, it's ideal for those keen on traditional Japanese ceramics. Bus to Ichijo-Modoribashi (see left) (10 am–4.30 pm, closed Monday, admission varies).

Map 7 GINKAKU-JI AREA
■ Ginkaku-ji Temple 銀閣寺
■ The Philosopher's Walk 哲学の道
■ Hashimoto Kansetsu Museum 橋本関雪記念館

Descend Mt Daimonji (see page 37) toward **Ginkaku-ji**, the Temple of the Silver Pavilion, and you will traverse an odd field full of fire-pits. This is where one of the giant flaming kanji characters is lit during the midsummer

Nijo Castle Garden

Daimonji-yaki Festival. Descend the mountain to find yourself at Ginkaku-ji (alternatively, begin the climb at Ginkaku-ji and conclude it at Nanzen-ji, page 37).

Ginkaku-ji, the Temple of the Silver Pavilion, was meant to be a counterpart to Kinkaku-ji (the Temple of the Golden Pavilion) but is lacking in silver due to 15th-century logistical issues (8.30 am–4.30 pm, ¥500). It's a lovely Zen temple with scenic moss and sand gardens and is more serene than the golden one across town. If you prefer strolling to hiking, you can also go from Ginkaku-ji to Nanzen-ji along **The Philosopher's Walk** (Tetsugaku no michi), a pleasant winding footpath along a canal lined with cherry trees. It's named in honor of Kitaro Nishida, a 20th-century Japanese philosopher who walked it daily for inspiration. Along or near the path are various temples and shrines and the **Hashimoto Kansetsu Museum**, a beautiful historic villa and former dwelling of Hashimoto Kansetsu, the Japanese painter who planted the cherry trees along the Philosopher's Walk (10 am–5 pm, ¥800).

Map 8 SHUGAKU-IN AND SHINSEN-DO AREA
■ Takaragaike Park 宝が池公園
■ Shugaku-in Rikyu 修学院離宮

Quiet and sedate and ringed by mountains, northern Kyoto features several sights, including Kyoto's most ancient shrines, a former Imperial villa and expansive parks and gardens. These are spread out and not ideal for walking about from place to place.

The sprawling **Takaragaike Park** is a good place for a walk or a picnic. It's centered on a pond 1.8 km (1.1 miles) in circumference, dug in the 18th century for rice crop irrigation. Popular with joggers, the park offers rowboats for rental at ¥1,000 per hour. It's only mildly marred by the architectural miscalculation that is the Kyoto International Conference Center. There's a strolling road through natural surroundings and a play zone for children, Kodomo-no-rakuen, designed to encourage physical exploration. A 10 minute walk from exit 5 of Kokusaikaikan Station (Karasuma subway line) or Takaragaike Station (Eizan Railway) or bus to Takaragaike stop (always open, free, Kodomo-no-rakuen open 9 am–4.30 pm).

To the east of Takaragaike Park, nestled up against the mountains, is **Shugaku-in Rikyu** (Shugaku-in Imperial Villa or Shugaku-in

Detached Palace), famed for its large, magnificent landscaped gardens. It was originally a nunnery before being turned into a retreat by Emperor Go-Mizuno'o after his abdication in the 17th century. The three gardens (Lower, Middle and Upper) make use of the principle of *shakkei* or "borrowed scenery," incorporating the backdrop of the surrounding mountains into their design, and feature ponds, teahouses, a waterfall and pathways for ambling. The view from the Upper Garden is spectacular. A 15 minute walk from Shugaku-in Rikyu-michi bus stop (Bus 5 from Kyoto Station) or a 25 minute walk toward the mountains from Shugaku-in Station (Eizan Line).

The Eizan Line itself, specifically the Kurama branch, is pleasant to ride in November or May because of its tunnel of maple leaves (see the section on Kurama Village, page 78).

Map 9 SHIMOGAMO AREA
■ Demachiyanagi Station 出町柳駅
■ Shimogamo-jinja Shrine 下鴨神社
■ Jotenkaku Art Museum 相国寺承天閣美術館
■ Shokoku-ji Temple 相国寺
■ Nishijin Textile Center 西陣織会館
■ Urasenke Chado Research Center 裏千家茶道資料館

Demachiyanagi Station is the terminus of the Keihan Line, serving the east side of Kyoto, its southern suburbs and the modern metropolis of Osaka about 45 minutes away. It's also the start and end point of the Eizan Railway through northern Kyoto, which branches off into two lines bound for Mt Hiei and Mt Kurama respectively.

Near Demachiyanagi, on the spear of land between the fork of the Kamo and Takano rivers, is **Shimogamo-jinja Shrine**. Dating back to prehistoric times, though the buildings themselves are somewhat newer, it honors Kyoto's creator and guardian deity and his daughter. Reach the shrine by a path through the lovely, environmentally protected Tadasu-no-mori woods. A 15 minute walk from Demachiyanagi Station or Bus 4 from Demachiyanagi to Shimogamojinja-mae.

To the west of the Kamo River fork is the **Jotenkaku Art Museum**, on the precincts of **Shokoku-ji Temple**, featuring treasures from nearby temples dating from the Muromachi Period (1337–1573, a zenith of Kyoto culture). Imadegawa Station (Karasuma subway line) or bus to Doshisha-mae (10 am–5 pm, ¥600).

The **Nishijin Textile Center** is a modern

building dedicated to the ancient traditions of the kimono and weaving, once a flourishing industry in this area. Visit if you have an interest in kimono or textiles; catch a kimono show or try your hand at hand-weaving. Or dress up as a *geiko* (geisha), *maiko* (apprentice geisha) or in a regular kimono. You can also rent a kimono for the day and walk around the city. The Center is about 10 blocks west of the northwest corner of Imperial Palace Park. Bus to Horikawa-Imadegawa stop (9 am–5 pm, free. Fees for activities vary). Make reservations for costume and hands-on activities: call 075-451-9231. The surrounding Nishijin district is a quiet one with traditional *machiya* townhouses remaining and remnants of the kimono and textile trade that once boomed here.

The **Urasenke Chado Research Center** is recommended for people interested in the tea ceremony. Its galleries have a replica tearoom and hold special exhibitions, but not always however (check www.urasenke.or.jp/ for updates). Bus to Horikawa Teranouchi bus stop (10 am–4 pm, ¥800, includes *matcha* tea and a sweet served to you).

Map 10 KAMIGAMO AREA

■ **Kamigamo Shrine** 上賀茂神社
■ **Kyoto Botanical Gardens** 京都府立植物園

Shimogamo-jinja Shrine (page 39) is part of a pair along with **Kamigamo Shrine**, which is even older, and in fact Kyoto's oldest shrine. (*shimo* and *kami* mean "lower" and "upper" respectively.) Kamigamo Shrine also features historic gates and buildings and is known for two intriguing symmetrical sand cones, part of an ancient purification ritual. A 15 minute walk from Kitayama Station (Karasuma subway line) or Bus 4 to Kamigamojinja-mae. Both shrines are among the 17 "Historic Monuments of Ancient Kyoto" designated as UNESCO World Heritage.

Located between the two are the **Kyoto Botanical Gardens**, which are among Japan's largest. It's a wonderful place for a stroll, with broad lawns, a tropical greenhouse and conservatory, a playground and over 10,000 kinds of trees, flowers and plants, including gardens of seasonal favorites like roses and cherry blossoms, as well as a fascinating arbor of oddly shaped gourds. Near Exit 3 of Kitayama Station (Karasuma subway line) or Bus 1 to Shokubutsuen-mae (9 am–5 pm, last entry 4 pm, ¥200).

Map 11 KINKAKU-JI AND DAITOKU-JI AREA

■ **Kinkaku-ji Temple** 金閣寺
■ **Daitoku-ji Temple** 大徳寺
■ **Daisen-in Temple** 大仙院
■ **Ryogen-in Temple** 龍源院
■ **Zuiho-in Temple** 瑞峰院
■ **Koto-in Temple** 高桐院
■ **Butsuden Hall** 仏殿
■ **Funaoka-yama** 船岡山
■ **Kitano Tenmangu Shrine** 北野天満宮

This area of Kyoto is largely quiet and residential but it has several major tourist attractions, including some of the most renowned Zen temples. The best known is **Kinkaku-ji**, the Temple of the Golden Pavilion, officially named Rokuon-ji. This Muromachi Period (1337–1573) Zen temple has lovely strolling gardens around a pond that reflects its centerpiece, the golden pavilion itself. Burned to the ground by a mentally unbalanced monk in 1950, it was rebuilt soon after, more radiant than ever, and looks magnificent year round but said to be best in the snow. The only drawback is that it can be packed. Try to go on a weekday or in the morning. Many buses go to Kinkakuji-michi stop (9 am–5 pm, ¥400).

A nice contrast can be found in **Daitoku-ji**, a sprawling and much less crowded Zen temple complex. Daitoku-ji is the name of both the entire complex and the largest of 20 plus temples. Those open to the public include **Daisen-in**, **Ryogen-in** and **Zuiho-in**, with celebrated Zen rock gardens, and **Koto-in**, with beautiful fall foliage during the season (around late November), plus the main **Butsuden Hall**. To wander around Daitoku-ji, it's best to be in a Zen state of mind and not in a hurry. Bus 101, 205 or 206 to Daitoku-ji-mae stop or a 15 minute walk from Kitao-ji Station, Karasuma subway line (9 am–4.30 pm or so depending on the sub-temple, ¥400 or so for individual temples).

Just south of Daitoku-ji is the somewhat ominous hillock of **Funaoka-yama**, where resides the Black Tortoise, northern guardian out of four protective spirits in the original feng shui-based layout of the city. Some say it's haunted or "charged" with spiritual energy. It's not necessarily a must-see spot, but there's a park with a nice view and it's a prime spot to watch the Daimonji-yaki Festival on August 16, in which giant kanji characters on five mountains around Kyoto are set aflame.

February in Kyoto can be bleak and cold

Ryoan-ji Temple

but it's the peak season for viewing plum blossoms. They're less famous than cherry blossoms but arguably even more beautiful, with an enchanting variety of colors and branch and petal shapes. The best place to see them in Kyoto is at **Kitano Tenmangu Shrine**, built in 947 to appease the spirit of brilliant scholar Sugawara no Michizane, unjustly exiled by political enemies. Because of his fondness for plum trees, they are found at the hundreds of Tenmangu shrines throughout Japan dedicated to Sugawara. He is the patron saint of students, who pray at Tenmangu shrines before exams. The plum grove of Kitano Tenmangu from mid-February through mid-March is a sea of white, pink, red and purple, and on February 25 a Plum Blossom Festival is held with a tea ceremony attended by *geiko* and *maiko* (geisha and apprentice geisha). Also on this day, and on the 25th of every month, is the **Tenjin-san flea market**, one of Kyoto's largest—perfect for finding unique gifts and souvenirs and trying Japanese street cuisine. The gardens also have maple trees that turn radiant colors around late November. Bus 50, 51, 55, 101, 102 or 203 to Kitanotenmangu-mae stop (free, 9 am–6 pm [5 pm Oct. through Mar.]).

Map 12 RYOAN-JI AREA

■ **Kitano Hakubai-cho Station** 北野白梅町駅
■ **Ryoan-ji Temple** 龍安寺
■ **Toei Kyoto Studio Park** 東映太秦映画村

Right next to the Kitano Tenmangu Shrine (above) is **Kitano Hakubai-cho Station** on the Keifuku Kitano Line, one of Kyoto's few remaining trams. It has a nostalgic atmosphere that makes it a fun ride in and of itself. Two stations on is **Ryoan-ji,** another marvelous Zen temple and home to perhaps the most famous rock garden of all. Its 15 rocks, resembling islands in a gravel sea, are arranged so that at least one is hidden from view no matter the viewing angle. Nestled among the temple's beautiful and spacious gardens are a large pond and a restaurant serving *yudofu* (tofu simmering in a hot pot with some vegetables and mushrooms), beer and saké, which you can enjoy while lounging on tatami mats and gazing out on the scenery. Keifuku Kitano Line to Ryoanji-michi Station, Bus 50 or 55 to Ritsumeikan Daigaku-mae or Bus 59 to Ryoanji stop (8 am–5 pm [8.30 am–4.30 pm, December–February], ¥500).

For a different sort of entertainment, visit **Toei Kyoto Studio Park** (aka Uzumasa

Eigamura), a theme park that's also a working set for samurai films and TV programs. Edo-period townscapes are recreated and you can see filming demonstrations as well as ninja performances, a ninja maze, a 360-degree 3D theater and a haunted house. For additional fees you can be dressed up in any of 30 period costumes. It's a good change of pace, especially for those with kids. Close to Uzumasa Station, Keifuku Arashiyama Line (9 am–5 pm [9.30–4.30 in winter], ¥2,200).

Map 13 ARASHIYAMA AREA

- ■ **Togetsu-kyo Bridge** 渡月橋
- ■ **Iwatayama Monkey Park** 嵐山モンキーパーク
- ■ **Tenryu-ji Temple** 天龍寺
- ■ **Sagano Bamboo Grove** 嵯峨野竹林
- ● **Okochi Sanso Villa** 大河内サンチョヴィラ
- ■ **Saga Toriimoto Preserved Street** 嵯峨鳥居本町
- ■ **Adashino Nenbutsu-ji Temple** 化野念仏寺
- ■ **Otagi Nenbutsu-ji Temple** 愛宕念仏寺
- ■ **Mt Atago** 愛宕山
- ■ **Gio-ji Temple** 祇王寺
- ■ **Nison-in Temple** 二尊院
- ■ **Jojakko-in Temple** 常寂光寺
- ■ **Suzumushi-dera Temple** 鈴虫寺
- ■ **Kokedera (Saiho-ji Temple)** 西芳寺

In far west Kyoto is Arashiyama-Sagano, one of the most scenic and popular districts in Kyoto. It's a bit off the beaten path but there is plenty to see, so devote a full day at least to this area.

From Arashiyama Station on the Hankyu or Keifuku lines, it's a short walk to the **Togetsu-kyo Bridge**, with a view of the mountains resplendent with fall foliage in autumn and cherry blossoms in spring. The bridge is the central landmark of the district.

You can rent bicycles outside the train stations for ¥800 per day or so. Or for more leisurely scenic enjoyment, take the **Sagano Scenic Railway**, a charming old-fashioned train that winds its way slowly along a ravine from Torokko Arashiyama Station about 30 minutes to Kameoka (no trains in January and February). From a pier near Kameoka Station, you can take the **Hozugawa River Cruise** back to Arashiyama by open, flat bottomed boat (about two hours, ¥1,700). Also, from the pier near Togetsu-kyo Bridge, you can get on a cormorant fishing (*ukai*) boat, departing daily at 7 am and 8 pm in July and August and at 6.30 am and 7.30 pm in early September. For another kind of encounter with the wild kingdom, visit **Iwatayama**

Monkey Park just south of the bridge. A short climb up the mountain will bring you close to over 100 free-roaming Japanese macaques. They're harmless, but don't show them food (9 am–5 pm [until 4 pm in winter], ¥550).

Sagano, north of the river, is less touristy. Coming to Arashiyama by the Keifuku Line, you'll arrive north of Togetsu-kyo Bridge. There's an open-air natural hot spring footbath at the station, well worth ¥150 in winter if you have tired feet. Across the street from the station is **Tenryu-ji**, one of Kyoto's greatest Zen temples, with magnificent landscape gardens to which the surrounding mountains form a "borrowed scenery" backdrop (8.30 am–5 pm or 5.30 pm, ¥500). Outside the north gate of Tenryu-ji to the left is the **Sagano Bamboo Grove**, entrancing with its dappled light and shade and rustling when a breeze blows. After 200 m (656 ft) the road through the grove comes to a T, and to the right is **Okochi Sanso Villa**, former home of silent film star Okochi Denjiro (1896–1962). A luxurious traditional private residence, it is an interesting contrast to temples and the like (9 am–5 pm, ¥1,000).

North of the grove are quiet lanes and fields. Wander through them up to **Saga Toriimoto Preserved Street**, a historic street of thatched-roof farmhouses and traditional townhouses, largely converted to shops and restaurants. The incline leads up to **Adashino Nenbutsu-ji Temple** and a few minutes further up the road, **Otagi Nenbutsu-ji Temple**. Both have thousands of stone Buddhist statues, those of the former representing the souls of the dead, and the moss-covered ones at the latter showing followers of Buddha, each with a different facial expression. You can continue hiking up the mountain, **Mt Atago**, Kyoto's highest at 924 m (3,000 ft). Climbing to the top and back is an all-day activity.

Elsewhere in Sagano, in addition to several other beautiful temples (**Gio-ji, Nison-in** and **Jojakko-ji**), is the rustic **Rakushisha cottage**, a must-see for haiku enthusiasts for its connection to poet Matsuo Basho. All in all, once you escape the touristy areas around the station, the Arashiyama-Sagano district is the ideal place to find the lost Japan of the past. It can be crowded during fall foliage and cherry blossom seasons and in December when the Hanatouro event is held (scenic streets are lined with lanterns and ikebana displays).

Other attractions in western Kyoto are the temples **Suzumushi-dera** (Cricket Temple)

(9 am–4 pm, ¥500 including tea and sweets) and **Kokedera** (Moss Temple, officially **Saiho-ji**), featuring the eponymous organisms. Kokedera is Kyoto's most expensive temple (¥3,000) and requires reservations made at least seven days in advance. Write to Saiho-ji Temple, 56 Jingatani-cho, Matsuo, Nishikyo-ku, Kyoto, 615-8286, Japan, with your name and address, number of people, date you want to visit and a self-addressed, stamped return postcard. The trouble and expense is meant to limit the number of visitors and protect the spectacular moss. Visitors also experience chanting and copying sutras. Both temples are a short bus ride from Matsuo Station on the Hankyu Line.

Map 14 TOFUKU-JI AND FUSHIMI-INARI AREA

■ **Fushimi-Inari Taisha Shrine** 伏見稲荷大社
■ **Tofuku-ji Temple** 東福寺
■ **To-ji Temple** 東寺

A bit further south is **Fushimi-Inari Taisha**, a major Shinto shrine dedicated to the harvest deity Inari. It is best known for its thousands of red *torii* gates forming a tunnel over the pilgrimage course that wanders through the woods behind the outer shrine. The inscriptions on the gates indicate that they were

Fushimi Inari Shrine

donated, often by local business people. You may notice pairs of guardian statues of foxes, which are considered the messengers of Inari. This is one shrine and scenic walk (2–3 hours to the top of a small mountain and back) that should not be missed even if you only have a few days to spend in Kyoto. Culinary adventurers may want to try the barbecued sparrows on skewers that are sold at shops on the walk up to the shrine from the station. Vegetarians can enjoy *inari-zushi* (rice wrapped in sweet fried tofu) or *kitsune udon* (noodles in broth with fried tofu), fried tofu being a favorite food of the fox. Keihan Line to Fushimi-Inari Station or JR Nara Line to Inari Station. (Always open, free.)

One station from Kyoto Station on the JR Nara Line, or one station south of Shichijo on the Keihan Line, is Tofuku-ji. This is home to **Tofuku-ji Temple,** a Zen temple that's one of the top spots in the city (or indeed anywhere in Japan) for maple leaf viewing. The fall foliage is usually at its most spectacular in late November and hordes descend on the peaceful and spacious temple grounds around this time. A Japanese nature appreciation event like this is a sight unto itself, with cell phone cameras whirring left and right as people seek the perfect shot. The leaves really are spectacular. Japanese maples are quite beautiful in May as well, when their leaves are at their freshest and most verdant. The temple is open all year round, with other attractions including the Hojo priestly quarters and rock gardens. (9 am–4.30 pm [hours vary slightly depending on the season], ¥400 for each of two separate viewing areas.)

Southwest of Kyoto Station is **To-ji Temple**, with its iconic five-storied pagoda, Japan's tallest. To-ji means "East Temple," and there was originally a West Temple, the two of which flanked the Rashomon gate (of Ryunosuke Akutagawa's story and Akira Kurosawa's film, no longer existent). On the 21st of each month, there is a large and popular **flea market** outside the temple, the perfect place to shop if you want to find some genuine artifacts of Japan and not just typical souvenir shop fare. On the first Sunday of each month is a smaller flea market for antiques only. To-ji Temple is on Kujo-dori, a 15 minute walk from Kyoto Station or 5 minutes from Toji Station on the Kintetsu Kyoto Line. (9.30 am–5.30 pm March–Sep., 9.30 am–4.30 Sep.–March, ¥500 or ¥800 on the infrequent occasions when the pagoda is open to the public.)

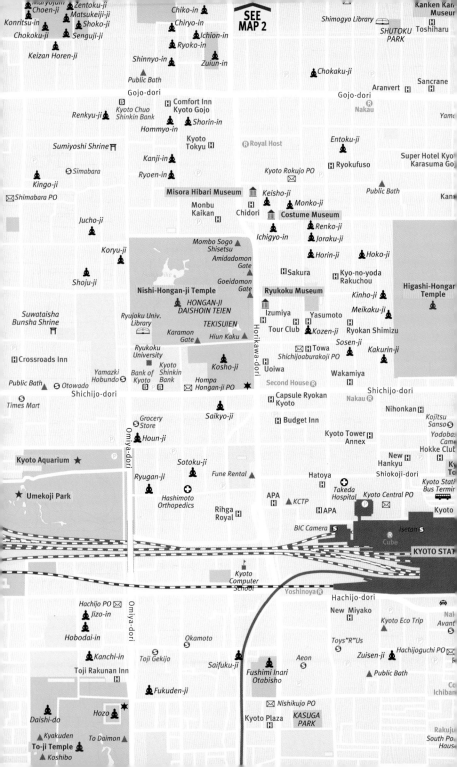

Map 1 Kyoto Station Area

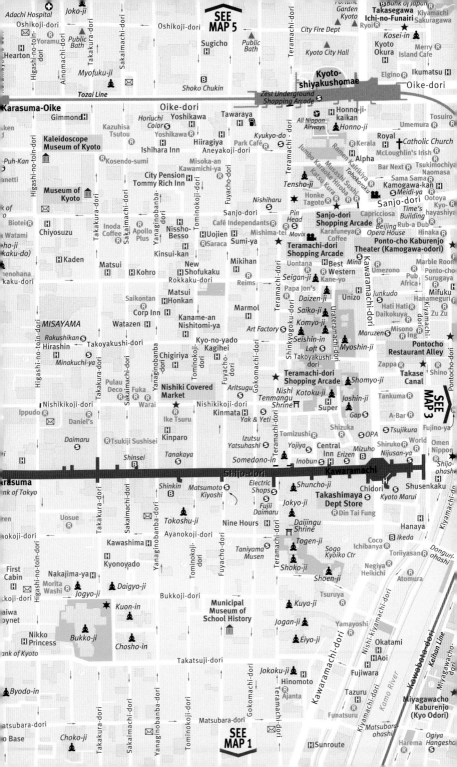

Demian H
Kongo-ji ⚲
Higashiyama
Big Week H

SEE MAP 4 ✉

Asuka ℝ Tozai Line
Higashiyama H

Sanjo-dori

Sanjo Hiromichi PO

Konchi-in ♨

Map 3 Gion and Kiyomizu Area

Hokekyo-in ♨

Keage

Ryoon-ji ⚲

Bukko-ji ♨

250 m
500 ft

Westin Miyako

N

Humans Well Kyoto

Awata Shrine ⛩

Jomyo-in ⚲
Sengu-in ⚲
Ryosho-in ⚲

Awatasanso H ⚲ Sonsho-in
⚲ Shoren-in

Shorenin Kyu Karigosho

Tomb of Hanazono Jurakuinnoue-no-misasagi ★

Niomon-dori

oku-in

MURAYAMA PARK

Chion-in ⚲

Kohojo

cho-michi

Shinju-in ⚲

Sotai-in ⚲

Ohojo   Saishido

Genko-in ⚲ ⚲
Kogen-in ⚲

Meido

Sammon

Isshin-in ⚲

Toju Wajun Kaikan

Tobu Koen Kanri Jimusho

Kyoto Yoshimizu ⚲
Anyo-ji ⚲

MARUYAMA PARK

Hotei Saami
H Kichu-an

Salon Haraguchi Tenseian

nabokokan H

★ ⚲ Chorakukan

Maruyama Park

Kyoto Maruyama Park Outdoor Music Stage

H ⚲ Senraku

Ryuchi Kaikan

naka

Maruyama Ongakudo

⚲ Sorin-ji

Shogunzuka ⚲

Daiun-in ⚲

Higashi-Otani

Choraku-ji ⚲

Tembodai ▲

ion Sano

⚲ Korin-in
H Ryokan
ℝ Motonago

Yoshinoya

⚲ Gesshin-ji

do

Bochi Jimusho

Kikunoi Inn

Higashi Otani Cemetery

Shoren-in Shogunzuka Dainichido

Higashiyama Dr. Way

⚲ Kodai-ji Sho Museum

Entoku-in H
Uemura

Kodai-ji Zen Temple

KODAIJI PARK

Shiei Tembodai ▲

HIGASHIYAMA SANCHO PARK

H Rikiya
nahan

an Uemura

Ryozen ⚲

Kodaiji Shikije

Homotsuden

Gokoku Shrine ⛩

Kodaiji Kannon ⚲

⛩ Saikan

Omen

ℝ Kodai-ji

Kodaiji-minamimonzen-dori

Ryozen Historical Museum

ℝ Bal Main
oh Higashiyama

ℝ Kyoyamato

Reimei Shrine

Wasaka-no-to (Hokan-ji Temple) ⚲
Konsenryu H
Ninen-zaka

⚲ Shoho-ji

Kashogama
ottery School ℝ

Maiko Henshin Studio Shiki
⚲ Kasagi-ya ℝ Doi
H Ladies Inn Sakata

Kasagi-ya ℝ

H Kiyomizu Sanso

H Ryozen

B&B GH

ashiyamaso

Saiko-ji H

ℝ Oblio
ℝ Kanojuan
Nishiri

H **Sannen-zaka**

Inoda Coffee

⚲ Kosho-ji

izu-zaka Shichimiya
o-ji

Akebonotei Iwai

ekurobutai H ★

omizu-zaka

★ Matsubara-dori

Shimpuku-ji ⚲
Gift Shops

Zenko-ji ⚲

Joju-in ⚲

Baikado
Gift Shops

Baizando

akiya
nn

Junsei ℝ

Kogetsuda

Kimura Oshida

Nio-mon
Jishin-in ⚲
Sai-mon

Banten-jima ⚲

Jishu ⛩ Shrine

Shimizu New Way Chawan-zaka
Kiyomizu Youth Hostel

Yoshida Seiendo

Sanju-no-to ⚲
Kyo-do ⚲

Asakura-do ⚲
Kaisan-do ⚲

⚲ Shaka-do
⚲ Amida-do

⚲ Myokendo

Kiyomizu-dera Temple

⚲ Okuno-in

kendo

⚲ Emmei-in

Otowa-no-taki Falls

zu-ji

TORIBEYAMA CEMETERY

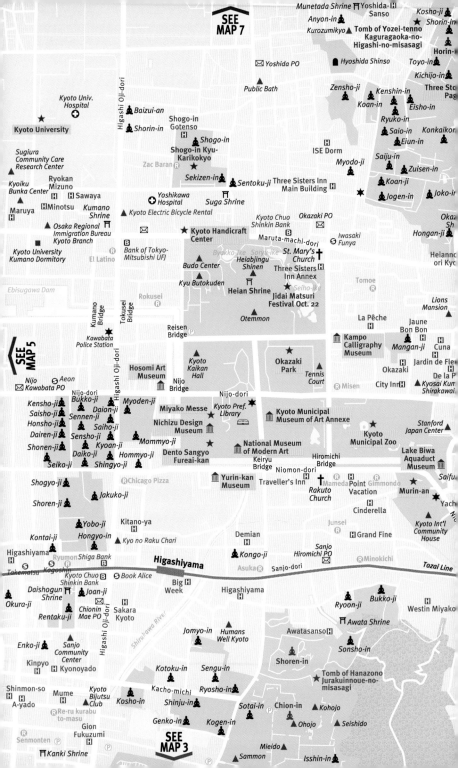

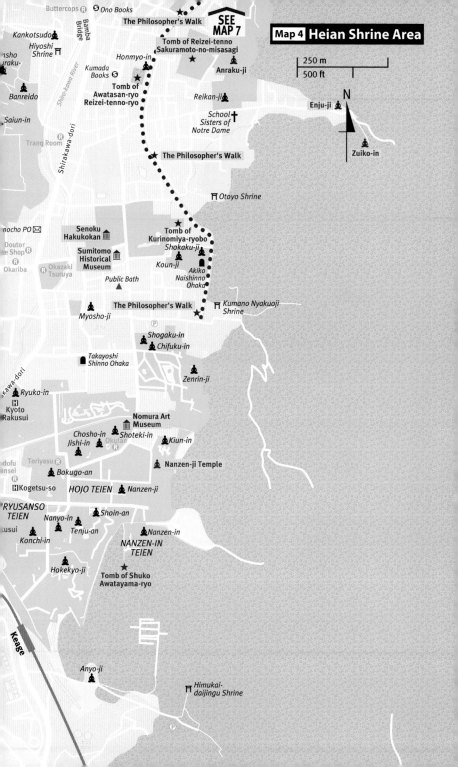

Buttercops **ⓡ** Ono Books
The Philosopher's Walk
Bamba Bridge
Kankotsudo **ⓡ**
Hiyoshi Shrine **卍**
sho raku-
SEE MAP 7
Map 4 Heian Shrine Area

Tomb of Reizei-tenno Sakuramoto-no-misasagi ★
Honmyo-in
ⓢ Kumada Books
Anraku-ji ★

250 m
500 ft

Tomb of Awatasan-ryo Reizei-tenno-ryo
Reikan-ji 卍
Enju-ji 卍
N

Banreido 卍
School Sisters of Notre Dame ✝
Zuiko-in 卍

Saiun-in

Shirakawa-dori
Shiro-kawa River

Trang Room **ⓡ**

The Philosopher's Walk

卍 *Otoyo Shrine*

nocho PO ✉
Senoku Hakukokan 🏛
Tomb of Kurinomiya-ryobo
Doutor Coffee Shop **ⓡ**
Sumitomo Historical Museum 🏛
Shokaku-ji 卍
Koun-ji 卍
Okariba **ⓡ**
Okazaki Tsuruya **ⓡ**
Akiko Naishinno Ohaka
Public Bath ▲

The Philosopher's Walk ★
Myosho-ji 卍
卍 *Kumano Nyakuoji Shrine*

Shogaku-in 卍
Ⓟ
Chifuku-in 卍

Takayoshi Shinno Ohaka ◼
Zenrin-ji 卍

kawa-dori
Ryuko-in 卍
Kyoto Rakusui 🅷
Nomura Art Museum 🏛
Chosho-in 卍
Jishi-in 卍
Shoteki-in 卍
Okutan **ⓡ**
Kiun-in 卍

dofu nsei **ⓡ**
Toriyasu **ⓡ**
Bokugo-an 卍
🅷 Kogetsu-so
HOJO TEIEN
Nanzen-ji 卍
Nanzen-ji Temple

RYUSANSO TEIEN
Nanyo-in 卍
Shoin-an 卍
usui
Konchi-in 卍
Tenju-an 卍
Nanzen-in 卍
NANZEN-IN TEIEN

Hokekyo-ji 卍
Tomb of Shuko Awatayama-ryo ★

Keage

Anyo-ji 卍

卍 *Himukai-daijingu Shrine*
Ⓟ

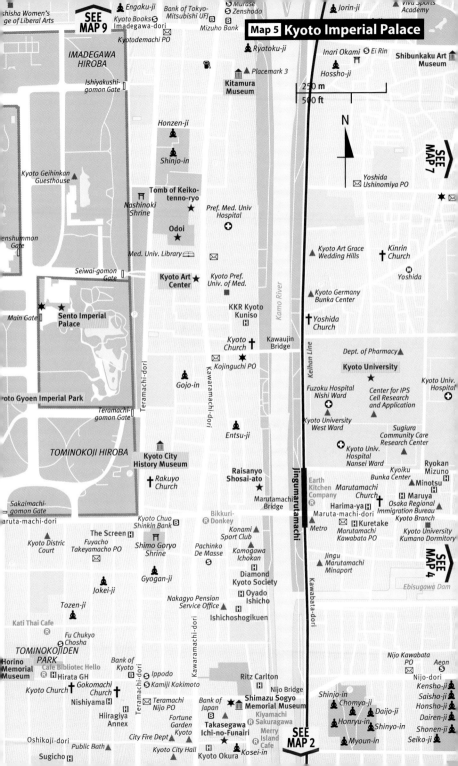

Map 5 Kyoto Imperial Palace

SEE
MAP 9

shisha Women's
ge of Liberal Arts

Engaku-ji
Kyoto Books
Imadegawa-dori

Bank of Tokyo-
Mitsubishi UFJ

Kyotodemachi PO

Murase
Zenshodo

Mizuho Bank

Jorin-ji

Viva Sports
Academy

Ryotoku-ji

Inari Okami   Ei Rin

Shibunkaku Art
Museum

IMADEGAWA
HIROBA

Hossho-ji

Ishiyakushi-
gomon Gate

Placemark 3

Kitamura
Museum

250 m

500 ft

N

Honzen-ji

Shinjo-in

Yoshida
Ushinomiya PO

SEE
MAP 7

Kyoto Geihinkan
Guesthouse

Tomb of Keiko-
tenno-ryo

Nashinoki
Shrine

Pref. Med. Univ
Hospital

Odoi

Med. Univ. Library

enshummon
Gate

Kyoto Art
Center

Kyoto Pref.
Univ. of Med.

Kyoto Art Grace
Wedding Hills

Kinrin
Church

Yoshida

Seiwai-gomon
Gate

Kyoto Germany
Bunka Center

Main Gate

Sento Imperial
Palace

KKR Kyoto
Kuniso

Yoshida
Church

Kamo River

Kawaujin
Bridge

Kyoto
Church

Kojinguchi PO

Gojo-in

Teramachi-dori

Kawaramachi-dori

Kelhan Line

Dept. of Pharmacy

Kyoto University

oto Gyoen Imperial Park

Fuzoku Hospital
Nishi Ward

Center for IPS
Cell Research
and Application

Kyoto Univ.
Hospital

Teramachi-
gomon Gate

Entsu-ji

Kyoto University
West Ward

TOMINOKOJI HIROBA

Kyoto City
History Museum

Raisanyo
Shosai-ato

Kyoto Univ.
Hospital
Nansei Ward

Sugiura
Community Care
Research Center

Rakuyo
Church

Marutamachi
Bridge

Kyoiku
Bunka Center

Ryokan
Mizuno

Minotsu

Sakaimachi-
gomon Gate

aruta-machi-dori

Earth
Kitchen
Company

Marutamachi
Church

Harima-ya

Maruya

Osaka Regional
Immigration Bureau
Kyoto Branch

Kyoto Chuo
Shinkin Bank

Bikkuri-
Donkey

Maruta-machi-dori

Metro

Kuretake
Marutamachi
Kawabata PO

Kyoto University
Kumano Dormitory

Jingumarutamachi

The Screen

Fuyacho
Takeyamacho PO

Shimo Goryo
Shrine

Konami
Sport Club

Pachinko
De Masse

Kamogawa
Ichokan

Jingu
Marutamachi
Minaport

SEE
MAP 4

Kyoto Distric
Court

Gyogan-ji

Diamond
Kyoto Society

Kawabata-dori

Ebisugawa Dam

Jokei-ji

Oyado
Ishicho

Tozen-ji

Nakagyo Pension
Service Office

Ishichoshogikuen

Kati Thai Cafe

Fu Chukyo
Chosha

Nijo Kawabata
PO

Aeon

TOMINOKOJIDEN
PARK

Cafe Bibliotec Hello

Hirata GH

Bank of
Kyoto

Nijo-dori

Horino
Memorial
Museum

Ippodo

Ritz Carlton

Kensho-ji

Kyoto Church

Gokomachi
Church

Kamiji Kakimoto

Nijo Bridge

Shinjo-in

Chomyo-ji

Saisho-ji

Nishiyama

Teramachi
Nijo PO

Bank of
Japan

Shimazu Sogyo
Memorial Museum

Daiji-ji

Honsho-ji

Hiiragiya
Annex

Fortune
Garden
Kyoto

Kiyamachi
Sakuragawa

Honryu-in

Shinyo-in

Dairen-ji

Shonen-ji

Oshikoji-dori

Public Bath

City Fire Dept

Takasegawa
Ichi-no-Funairi

Merry
Island
Cafe

Myoun-ji

Seiko-ji

Sugicho

Kyoto City Hall

Kyoto Okura

Kosei-ji

SEE
MAP 2

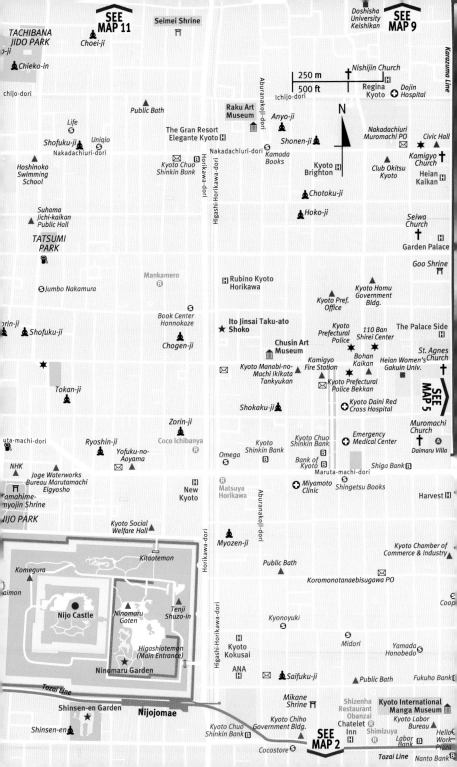

SEE MAP 8

Fukuzo-ji

Kitaoji Hospital

SEE MAP 9

Kyoto Univ. Fukui Kenichi Kinen Kenkyu Center

HIGASHIBIRAKI JIDO PARK

Tatekura Bridge

Myosei-ji

Sakyo Library

Takano Higashibiraki PO

Higashi Oji-dori

Chayama

Mugeko-in

TAKAHARA JIDO PARK

Tanaka Takahara PO

Kyoto University of Art and Design

Public Bath

Shuko-ji

Mototanaka

Kotaku-ji

Tanaka Shrine

Tanakahi-no-kuchi PO

Bank of Kyoto

Kyoto Shinkin Bank

Mikage-dori

Kitashirakawa Church

Eizan-Eizan Line

Jomyoan

Seisenkan Nakamura

Higashi Oji-dori

Kyoto Univ. Farm.

Kyoto Univ. Ground

Yosei Library

Dokusho-ji

Grace Tanaka

Kyoto Chuo Shinkin Bank

Dept. of Science

Monko-ji

Daini Central Hospital

KYOTO UNIVERSITY

Yukawa Kinenkan

Kofuku-ji

Research Inst. for Applied Sci.

Jusen-in

Louis Pasteur Center for Medical Research

Tomb of Kakunomiya-ryobo

Dept. of Agriculture

Dept. of Science Botanical Garden

Viva Sports Academy

Sunny Place

Ryuken-in

Chikuso-in

Chion-ji

Nyoi-ji

Dept. of Science

Tomb of Gonijo-tenno Kitashirakawa-no-misasagi

Sukiya

Parlor Monaco

Yogen-in

Imadegawa-dori

Daikoku

B&B Juno

Grott

Shibunkaku Art Museum

Kyoto University Gym

Higashi Oji-dori

Dept. of Engineering

Institute for Research in Humanities

YOSHIDAYAMA PARK

Mt. Yoshida

Kyoto University Museum

Kansai Nichifutsu Gakka

Dept. of Law

Dept. of Literature

SEE MAP 5

Mausoleum Honoring Empress Go-murakami

Dept. of Edu

Kyoto University

France

Library

Dept. of Economics

Dept. of Engineering

Tomb of Daigo-tenno Kotaishi Yasuyorio-ohoka

Kyoto Univ. Inst. for Research in Humanities

Yoshida Shrine

Takenaka Inari-sha Shrine

Yoshida Gakudo

Sanin Shrine

Reimei Kyokai

Dept. of Integrated Human Studies

Daigen-gu Shrine

Yoshida

Dept. of Med.

Kyoto University

Tomb of Goichijo-tenno Bodaijuin-no-misasagi

Tohoku-in

Munetada Shrine

Yoshida-Sanso

Kosho-ji

Anyon-in

Tomb of Yozei-tenno

Shorin-in

Kurozumikyo

Kaguragaoka-no-Higashi-no-misasagi

Horin-in

SEE MAP 4

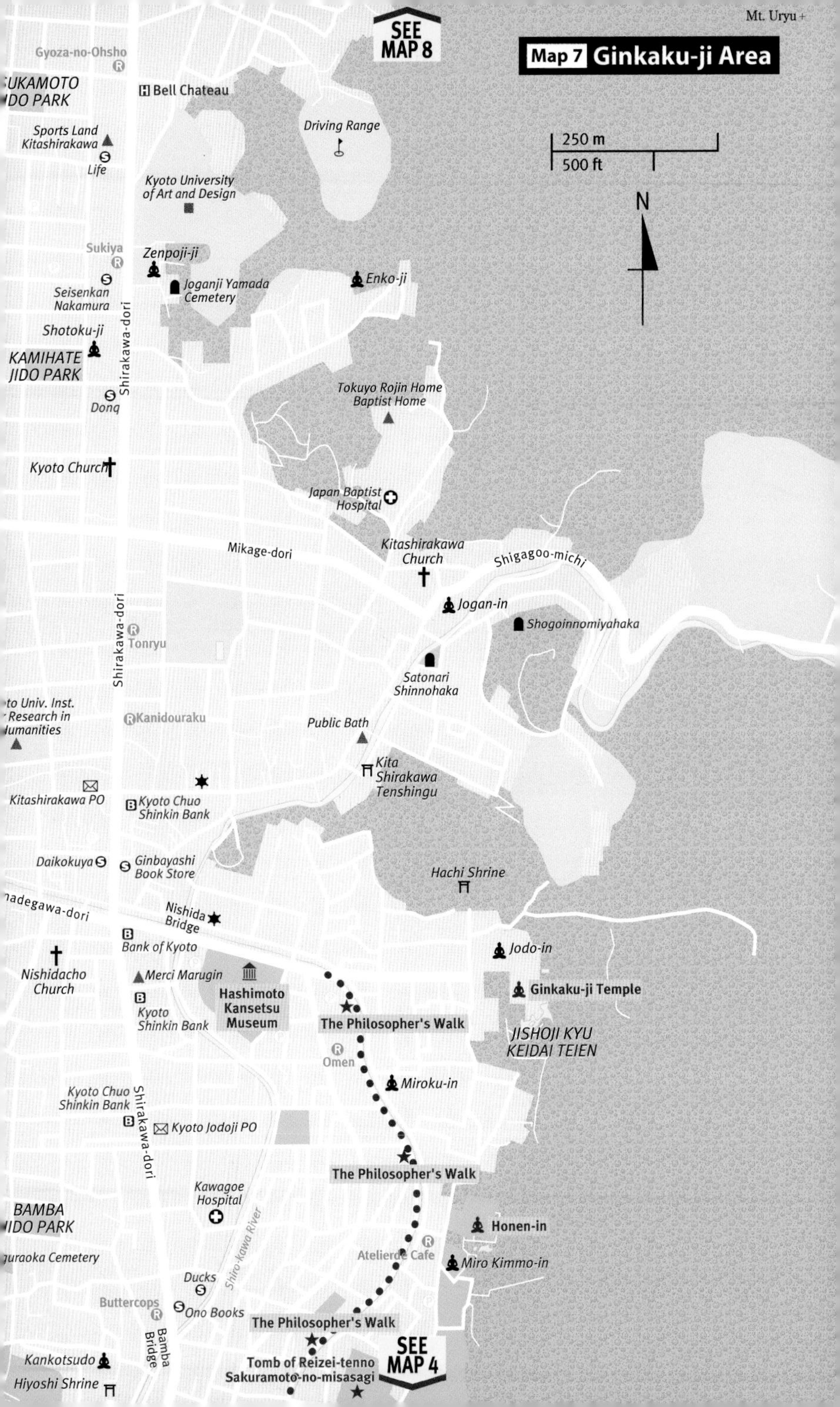

SEE MAP 8

Map 7 Ginkaku-ji Area

250 m
500 ft

N

Gyoza-no-Ohsho Ⓡ

ⓈUKAMOTO
ⒿIDO PARK

Ⓗ Bell Chateau

Sports Land
Kitashirakawa ▲

Ⓡ Life

Kyoto University
of Art and Design ▪

Driving Range

Sukiya Ⓡ

Zenpoji-ji

Ⓢ

Seisenkan
Nakamura

Shotoku-ji

KAMIHATE
ⒿIDO PARK

Joganji Yamada
Cemetery

Enko-ji

Ⓡ Dong

Kyoto Church ✛

Tokuyo Rojin Home
Baptist Home ▲

Japan Baptist
Hospital ✚

Mikage-dori

Kitashirakawa
Church ✟

Shigagoo-michi

Jogan-in

Shogoinnomiyahaka ▪

Shirakawa-dori

Ⓡ Tonryu

Satonari
Shinnohaka ▪

to Univ. Inst.
Research in
ⓊUmanities ▲

Ⓡ Kanidouraku

Public Bath

Kita
Shirakawa
Tenshingu 🏮

Kitashirakawa PO ✉

★

Ⓑ Kyoto Chuo
Shinkin Bank

Daikokuya Ⓢ

Ⓢ Ginbayashi
Book Store

Hachi Shrine 🏮

ⓝadegawa-dori

Nishida
Bridge ★

Ⓑ Bank of Kyoto

Nishidacho ✟
Church

▲ Merci Marugin

🏛 Hashimoto
Kansetsu
Museum

Jodo-in

Ginkaku-ji Temple

JISHOJI KYU
KEIDAI TEIEN

Ⓑ Kyoto
Shinkin Bank

The Philosopher's Walk ★

Ⓡ Omen

Kyoto Chuo
Shinkin Bank
Ⓑ

Miroku-in

✉ Kyoto Jodoji PO

Shirakawa-dori

Kawagoe
Hospital ✚

The Philosopher's Walk ★

BAMBA
ⒿIDO PARK

Honen-in

Ⓡ Atelier de Cafe

Miro Kimmo-in

ⓊUraoka Cemetery

Buttercops

Ducks

Ⓢ Ono Books

The Philosopher's Walk ★

Kankotsudo ▲

Bamba
Bridge

Tomb of Reizei-tenno
Sakuramoto-no-misasagi ★

SEE
MAP 4

Hiyoshi Shrine 🏮

Shiro-kawa River

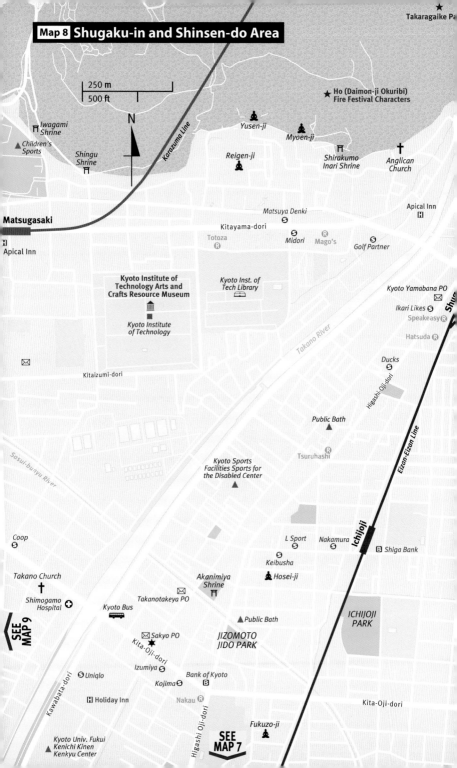

Map 8 Shugaku-in and Shinsen-do Area

★ Takaragaike Pa...

250 m
500 ft

N

⛩ Iwagami Shrine
▲ Children's Sports
Shingu Shrine ⛩

Karazuma Line

🧘 Yusen-ji
🧘 Myoen-ji
★ Ho (Daimon-ji Okuribi) Fire Festival Characters

🧘 Reigen-ji
⛩ Shirakumo Inari Shrine
✝ Anglican Church

Matsugasaki

Apical Inn 🏨

Matsuya Denki 🖥
Kitayama-dori
Totoza ®
Midori 🖥   ® Mago's
Golf Partner 🖥

Apical Inn 🏨

Apical Inn

Kyoto Institute of Technology Arts and Crafts Resource Museum 🏛
Kyoto Inst. of Tech Library 📖
Kyoto Institute of Technology 🏛

Kyoto Yamabana PO ✉
Ikari Likes 🖥
Speakeasy ®
Hatsuda ®

Shu...

Takano River

✉
Kitaizumi-dori

Ducks 🖥

Higashi-Oji-dori

Public Bath ▲

Sosui-bunyu River

Tsuruhashi ®

Eizan-Eizan Line

Coop 🖥

Kyoto Sports Facilities Sports for the Disabled Center

L Sport 🖥   Nakamura 🖥
Keibusha
🧘 Hosei-ji
Ichijoji
🅱 Shiga Bank

Takano Church ✝
Shimogamo Hospital ✚

Akanimiya Shrine ⛩

✉ Takanotakeya PO
Kyoto Bus 🚌

ICHIJOJI PARK

▲ Public Bath

JIZOMOTO JIDO PARK

◀ SEE MAP 9

✉ Sakyo PO ★
Kita-Oji-dori
Izumiya 🖥

🖥 Uniqlo
Kojima 🖥
🏨 Holiday Inn

Bank of Kyoto 🅱
Nakau ®

Kita-Oji-dori

Kawabata-dori

SEE MAP 7

🧘 Fukuzo-ji

Kyoto Univ. Fukui Kenichi Kinen Kenkyu Center

Higashi Oji-dori

Sekizan-zen-in

Kinokuniya

Yokuryu
Chi

Kyusuitei

★ Shugaku-in Rikyu Villa

Rinutei

Zenke-in

Heihachi
Tea House Inn

Kimyo-in

Shugakuin
Church

Donyu-ji

Rinkyu-ji

Otawa-gawa River

Kansai
Seminar
House

kuinrikyu-michi

Kyoto
University

nk of Kyoto
Shugaku
Kin Chu
kuin
pital
Ducks

Shiomi Hyakkaten

Saginomori
Shrine

Manshu-in

Takeda Yakuhin
Kogyo Kyoto Yakuyo
Shokubutsuen

yama
rgery

Kokusai
Condominium

Ichijoji Kita
Cemetery

Interna Ueda

Yakushido

Seiken-in

Public Bath

Hayama Itto-ji

Saien-ji

ankyu
Oasis

Kami-ichijoji
Public Hall

Enko-ji

Kyoto Chuo
Shinkin Bank

chinko
mega

Kyotoichijoji PO

Sasagawa
Kozo Shoten

Shomyo-ji

Nobotoke-an

JIDO
RK

Shisen-do

★

Hachidai
Shrine

ikuya
Sakai

Hongan-ji
Kitayama Betsuin

Tanukidani
Fudoin

Konpuku-ji

Namikiri
Fudo Myoo

Tanukidanisan
Fudoin

Ishikawa
Jozan Haka

SEE
MAP 7

Mt. Uryu +

Shirakawa-dori

Shirakawa-dori

Manju-in-dori

Ichijoji-michi

Shirakawa-dori

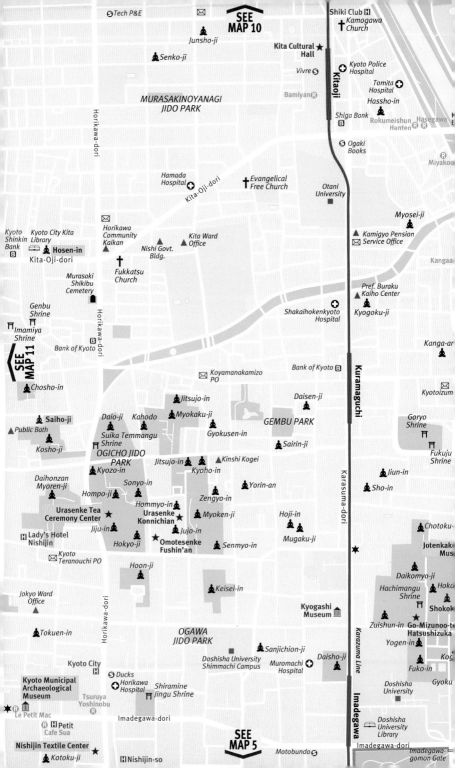

S Tech P&E

✉

SEE MAP 10

Shiki Club H

🔥 Junsho-ji

✝ Kamogawa Church

🔥 Senko-ji

Kita Cultural Hall ★

Vivre S

Kitaoji

Kyoto Police Hospital ✚

Tomita Hospital ✚

Hassho-in 🔥

MURASAKINOYANAGI JIDO PARK

Bamiyan Ⓡ

Shiga Bank B

Rokumeishun 🔥 Hanten Ⓡ Ⓡ Hasegawa Ⓡ

Miyako Ⓡ

Hamada Hospital ✚

Kita-Oji-dori

✝ Evangelical Free Church

Otani University ■

S Ogaki Books

Myosei-ji 🔥

Kyoto Shinkin Bank B

Kyoto City Kita Library 📖

🔥 Hosen-in

Kita-Oji-dori

✉ Horikawa Community Kaikan

Nishi Govt. Bldg.

🔺

Kita Ward Office ■

🔺 Kamigyo Pension

✉ Service Office

Kangae

Murasaki Shikibu Cemetery ■

✝ Fukkatsu Church

Horikawa-dori

Pref. Buraku 🔺 Kaiho Center

Kyogoku-ji 🔥

Genbu Shrine

Shakaihokenkyoto Hospital ✚

Kanga-ar

🔥 Kyotoizum

🏮 Imamiya Shrine

SEE MAP 11

Bank of Kyoto

Koyamanakamizo ✉ PO

Bank of Kyoto B

Goryo Shrine

🔥 Chosho-in

🔥 Jitsujo-in

🔥 Myokaku-ji

Daisen-ji 🔥

GEMBU PARK

Kuramaguchi

Karasuma-dori

Fukuju Shrine 🏮

🔥 Saiho-ji

Daio-ji 🔥 Kahodo 🔥

🔥 Jiun-ji

🔥 Sho-in

🔺 Public Bath

Suika Temmangu 🔥 Shrine

Gyokusen-in 🔥

Sairin-ji 🔥

Kosho-ji 🔥

OGICHO JIDO PARK 🏮

Jitsujo-in 🔥

🔺 Kinshi Kogei

Kyoho-in 🔥

Daihonzan 🔥 Myoren-ji

🔥 Kyozo-in

Sonyo-in 🔥

🔥 Yorin-an

Zengyo-in 🔥

Hoji-in 🔥

🔥 Chotoku-

Urasenke Tea 🔥 Ceremony Center

Hompo-in 🔥

Hommyo-in 🔥

Urasenke ★ Konnichian

🔥 Myoken-ji

Mugaku-ji 🔥

Jotenka Mus

H Lady's Hotel Nishijin

Jiju-in ★ 🔥

Jujo-in ★ 🔥

Omotesenke Fushin'an

Senmyo-in 🔥

★

Daikomyo-ji 🔥

🔥 Hoka

Hokyo-ji ★ 🔥

Hachimangu 🔥 Shrine

✉ Kyoto Teranouchi PO

Hoon-ji 🔥

Zuishin-in 🔥

Go-Mizunoo-te Hatsushizuka ★

Shokole 🔥

Jokyo Ward Office 🔺

Keisei-in 🔥

Yogen-in 🔥

Fuko-in 🔥

🔥 Tokuen-in

Kyogashi Museum 🏛

OGAWA JIDO PARK

Koٍ

Kyoto City H

S Ducks

Sanjichion-ji 🔥

Daisho-ji 🔥

Doshisha University

Gyoku

Kyoto Municipal Archaeological Museum 🏛

S Horikawa Hospital

Shiramine Jingu Shrine 🏮

Doshisha University Shimmachi Campus

Muromachi Hospital ✚

Doshisha University Library 📖

Tsuruya Yoshinobu 🏛

★ Ⓡ 🏛

Le Petit Mac

Imadegawa-dori

Imadegawa

Imadegawa-gomon Gate

Ⓡ H Petit Cafe Sua

SEE MAP 5

Nishijin Textile Center

🔥 Kotoku-ji

H Nishijin-so

Motobundo S

Imadegawa-dori

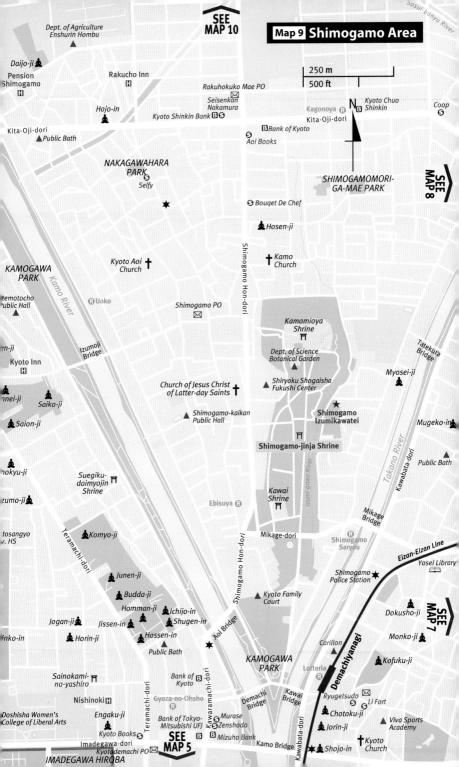

Okui

Mt. Komaru
137m

Public Bath

Kyoto Golf Club
(Kamigamo Course)

Daitoku-ji-dori

Noriaki
Maru Silk

MG

Fuji

Shingu
Shrine

Kamigamo
Shrine

Jinko-in

Kamo-kaido H'way

Ri-ibon

Aoi House

Katayama
Miko Shrine

Futabainari
Shrine

★

Kaocik

Wanwan

Boutique

Misono

Yamashita Hiroshi
Sakae Hall

Omiya-dori

Jinba Do

Misono
Bridge

Suzukimando

Nabesen

Kyoto Chuo
Shinkin Bank

Jigen-ji

Tenkaippin
Honbu

Saisenkan
Nakamura

Rozannu

Misono

Kamo River

Carlton Terrace

Sainen-ji

Kameya

Koryo
Museum of Art

Inokuma-dori

OMIYA
TRAFFIC
PARK

Kyonogano

Kamigamo
Bridge

Kyosushizen

Gen-i-dori

Kuga
Shrine

Ushiwaka-dori

Omiya-dori

Cafe Doji

Gourmet City

Murasaki Books

Hoonsha

Drug Land Hikari

★

Toho Books

Bank of Kyoto

Kyoto-Kita PO

Ishi
Shr

Green Gables

Jotoku-ji

Ogawa

Berubimoa

Shichiku-kita-dori

Funaoka Higashi-dori

Kitayama-dori

Patishiesumino

MG

Maki
Kitayama

Horikawa-dori

Kachan

Kyoto Chuo
Shinkin Bank

Omoto

Nishimura

Gokoku-ji

Kyoto Fukita
Police Station

Uekawa

Ueno-dori

Koyama Catholic
Church

Royal Host

Konen-ji

Shichiku-minami-dori

So Shrine

Shiun-ji

Pepekawashima
Matsunoki Pharmacy

SEE
MAP 11

Midori

Tech P&E

Junsho-ji

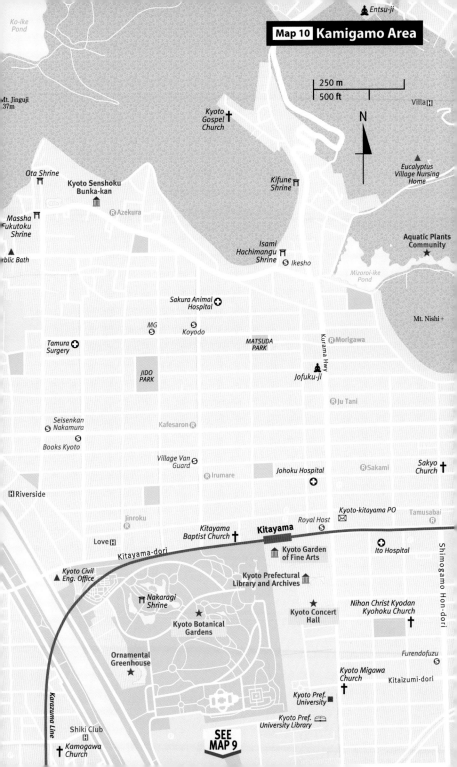

Map 10 Kamigamo Area

Map 11 Kinkaku-ji and Daitoku-ji Area

250 m
500 ft

N

Joshin-ji

Kinkaku
Akupunktur

Joshu-ji

Funeral Hall

Mt. Daimonji
+

Hidari-daimonji
(Daimon-ji Okuribi)
Fire Festival Characters

Eire

Carmelite
Monastery

Tomb of Sanjo-tenno
Kitayama-no-misasagi

Kyoto Seieikai

Fushigi Fudoin

Fumon-ji

Silver Home
Kinugasa

Tenmon-in

Tenryujin
Okami

Friends World
College

Ammimitaku

Kinugasa Church

Rokuon-ji
(Kinkaku-ji)
Garden

Kinkaku-ji Temple

Kurama-
guchi-dori

Kyoko-chi

Ritsumeikan Univ.
Dept. of Int'l Related

Kitayama
Bunko

Kinkaku

Hoon-ji
Bank of Kyoto

Kinagusa PO

Tomb of Shirakawa-
tenno-kasozuka

Hontsuji-dori

Shikichi
Shrine

Tomb of Kazan-tenno-
Kamiyanohotori-no-misasag

Mt. Kinugasa
+

Tomb of Gosuzaku-
tenno-Kasozuka

Tomb of
Kiyomorizuka

Rakuyo
Church

Yofuku-no-Aoyama

Gyu-kaku

Insho-Domoto
Museum of Fine Art

Yakiniku
Ichiba

Kyoto Chuo
Shinkin Bank

Kinukake-no-michi

Kura Sushi

Hachiman Shrine

Nishioji-dori

Joy

Gym

Coop

Art Research Ctr

Kyoto Museum
for World Peace

Chrysantheme

Od

Ritsumeikan
University

Seisenkan
Nakamura

Hirano Shrine

Kyoto
Komatsubara PO

Sato

Kit
Tenman
Sh

Senju-in

Koun-in

Toji-in

Shogen-ji

KOMATSUBARA
JIDO PARK

Seito

Od

Nishioji-dori

Tomb of Nijo-tenno
Koryuji-no-misasagi

Kagonoya

Tomb of
Hokyojimiya-ryobo

Shinnyo-ji

Kumano
Shrine

Arisan

St. Joseph Medical
Welfare Center

Rokusho
Shrine

TOJIIN JIDO
PARK

SEE
MAP 12

Bai

Public Bath

Kontai-ji

Higashimuki
Kannon-ji

SEE
MAP 12

Tanpopo

Senbon-dori

Kitayama-dori

Saiko-ji

Imamiya Shrine

Kazariya Ⓡ

Funaoka Higashi-dori

Ueno-dori

Shiun-ji

SEE MAP 10

Matsunoki Pharmacy

Midori

Isshin-ji

Onsendo

Hoshun-in
Ryusen-an

Daisen-in Temple

★ Daisen-in Garden

Raiko-ji

Nyoi-an

Shinju-an

Ryusho-ji
Jukoin Garden ★

Bukkyo University

Koho-an

Soken-in

Juko-in

Shumu Honsho

Yuimyo-ji

Koho-an Garden ★

Koto-in Temple

Sangen-in

Daitokuji Ikkyu

Shoju-in

Shogaku-ji

Public Bath

Daitoku-ji Temple

Korin-in

★ Butsuden Hall

Gyokurin-in

Zuiho-in Temple

Ryogen-in Temple

Daikyo-ji

Ryuko-in

Izusen Ⓢ

Daiji-in

Obai-in

Tokuzen-ji

Ichima
Ⓡ

Tombuyo Rojin Home Murasakino

Tani House

Yotoku-in

Daitokuji Ikkyu Ⓡ

Tomb of Goreizei-tenno-kasozuka ★

Pachinko Yodel

Kita-Oji-dori

Daiko-in

MG Ⓢ

Kyoto Shinkin Bank
Ⓑ

Volks Ⓡ

Kitaoji ✉ Sembon PO

Rakushi Public Hall

Kyoto Lite House

Unrin-in

Gakusai Kenkyusho Fuzoku Hospital ✚

Tomb of Konoe-tenno-kasozuka ★

Shingon-in

FUNAOKA PARK

Murasakino-kaikan Public Hall

Wakamiya Shrine

Imamiya Shrine

MIYAGAWA PARK

Funaoka-yama ★

Takeisao Shrine

Jotoku-ji ✉

SEE MAP 9

Jobon Rendai-ji

KAMIKASHIWANO PARK

Shamusho

Mercado Funaoka Ⓢ

Choken-ji

Chosho-in

Hosen-in

Matsunoki

UGASA AMIMICHI

Odoi K★

Pachinko Tamachan

Public Bath

Public Bath

Injo-ji

Senbon-dori

Tokuju-in

Shinkyo-ji

Fukusho-in

Daiko-ji

Gyoza-no-Ohsho Ⓡ

Joko-ji

Shonen-ji

Inryu-ji

Choei-ji

SHIMOKASHIWANO JIDO PARK

Zempuku-ji

Lady's Hotel Nishijin Ⓗ

Public Bath

Muryo-ji

Sembon Deranouchi PO ✉

Drug Land Hikari Ⓢ

Shakuzo-ji

Honzui-ji

Orinasu-kan Handmade Fabrics Museum

Kyoto Chuo Shinkin Bank Ⓑ

Nishijin Hospital Nishikan ✚

Nishijin Hospital ✚

Zuiun-in

Honkyu-ji

Kamigyo Hospital

Uho-in

Reihoden

Tamabuchi-dera

Hompo-in

Daihoon-ji

Shoju-in

Honryu-ji

Zeko-in

Hinjo-in

Shoman-ji

Ramen Kyoto Tengu

Zensho-ji

Shinnen-ji

Jozen-ji

Tomb of Hanshuin-ryo ★

Hanshu-in

Kura Sushi

Le Petit Mac ★

Shamusho

Tomyo-ji

Benrido Books

Kyoto Shinkin Bank Ⓑ

Saiho Ni-ji

Jodo-in

Imadegawa-dori

motsuden

Kitano PO ✉

Nishijin PO ✉

Imadegawa-dori

Honko-ji

Bank of Kyoto Ⓑ

Gonen-ji
Morianshindo Books

Bank of Tokyo-Mitsubishi UFJ Ⓑ

SEE MAP 6

Imadegawa-dori

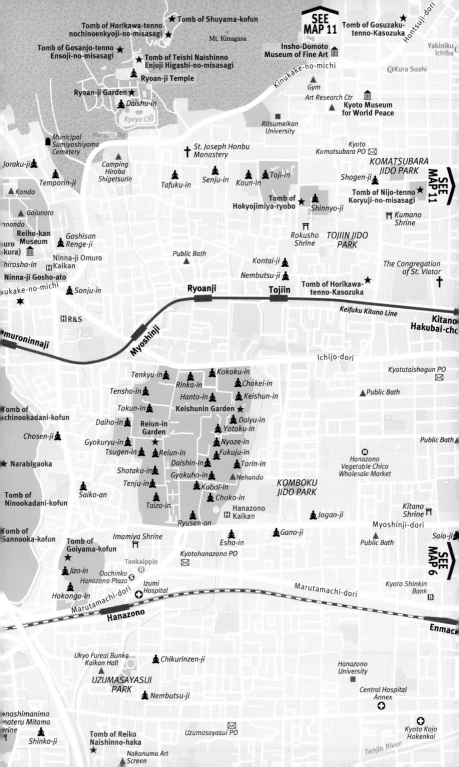

★ Tomb of Shuyama-kofun

Tomb of Horikawa-tenno
nochinoenkyoji-no-misasagi ★

Mt. Kinugasa

SEE MAP 11

★ Tomb of Gosuzaku-tenno-Kasozuka

Hontsuji-dori

Yakiniku
Ichiba

Insho-Domoto
Museum of Fine Art 🏛

Tomb of Gosanjo-tenno
Ensoji-no-misasagi ★

Kinukake-no-michi

Ⓡ Kura Sushi

Tomb of Teishi Naishinno
Enjoji Higashi-no-misasagi ★

Gym

Art Research Ctr 🏛

Kyoto Museum
for World Peace

Ryoan-ji Temple

🔆 Daishu-in

Ryoan-ji Garden ★

Ritsumeikan
University

Kyoyo Chi

Honda-Ike

Municipal
Sumiyoshiyama
Cemetery

† St. Joseph Honbu
Monastery

Kyoto
Komatsubara PO ✉

KOMATSUBARA
JIDO PARK

Joraku-ji 🔆

Camping
Hiroba
Shigetsurin

Senju-in 🔆

Toji-in 🔆

Shogen-ji 🔆

SEE MAP 11

Temporin-ji 🔆

Tafuku-in 🔆

Koun-in 🔆

Tomb of Nijo-tenno
Koryuji-no-misasagi ★

▲ Kondo

Tomb of
Hokyojimiya-ryobo 🔆

Shinnyo-ji

🔆 Kumano
Shrine

▲ Gojunoto

Shinnyo-ji 🔆

Reiho-kan
Museum 🏛

Goshisan
Renge-ji 🔆

Rokusho
Shrine 🏮

TOJIIN JIDO
PARK

iroshi-in

Ninna-ji Omuro
Kaikan 🅷

Public Bath
▲

Kontai-ji 🔆

The Congregation
of St. Viator †

Ninna-ji Gosho-ato

Nembutsu-ji 🔆

ukake-no-michi

🔆 Sonju-in

Ryoanji

Tojiin

Tomb of Horikawa-
tenno-Kasozuka ★

★

🅷 R&S

Keifuku Kitano Line

Kitano
Hakubai-cho

muroninnaji

Myoshinji

Ichijo-dori

Kyototaishogun PO ✉

Tenkyu-in 🔆

🔆 Kokoku-in

▲ Public Bath

Tensho-in 🔆

Rinka-in 🔆

🔆 Chokei-in

Tomb of
chinookadani-kofun

Tokun-in 🔆

Hanto-in 🔆

🔆 Keishun-in

Keishunin Garden ★

Daiho-in 🔆

🔆 Daiyu-in

Yotoku-in 🔆

Public Bath

Chosen-ji 🔆

Reiun-in
Garden

🔆 Nyoze-in

Hanazono
Vegetable Chico
Wholesale Market Ⓜ

★ Narabigaoka

Gyokuryu-in 🔆

Reiun-in 🔆

Fukuju-in 🔆

Kitano
Shrine 🏮

Tsugen-in 🔆

Daishin-in 🔆

🔆 Torin-in

Myoshinji-dori

Tomb of
Ninookadani-kofun

Shotaku-in 🔆

Gyokuho-in 🔆

▲ Nehando

KOMBOKU
JIDO PARK

Saio-ji

Saiko-an 🔆

Tenju-in 🔆

🔆 Kobai-in

SEE MAP 6

Tomb of
Sannooka-kofun

🔆 Choko-in

Public Bath

Taizo-in 🔆

Hanazono
Kaikan 🅷

🔆 Jogan-ji

Ryusen-an 🔆

🔆 Gano-ji

Public Bath

Tomb of
Goiyama-kofun

Imamiya Shrine 🏮

Esho-in 🔆

Kyotohanazono PO ✉

Kitano Shinkin
Bank Ⓑ

Tenkaippin Ⓡ

Jizo-in 🔆

Oachinko
Hanazono Plaza Ⓢ

Izumi
Hospital ✛

Marutamachi-dori

Kyoto Shinkin
Bank Ⓑ

Hokongo-in 🔆

Marutamachi-dori

Hanazono

Enmac

Ukyo Fureai Bunka
Kaikan Hall

🔆 Chikurinzen-ji

Hanazono
University

UZUMASAYASUI
PARK

🔆 Nembutsu-ji

Central Hospital
Annex ✛

noshimanima
nateru Mitama
rine

Uzumasayasui PO ✉

Kyoto Kojo
Hokenkai ✛

Shinko-ji 🔆

Tomb of Reiko
Naishinno-haka ★

Nakanuma Art
Screen ▲

Tenjin River

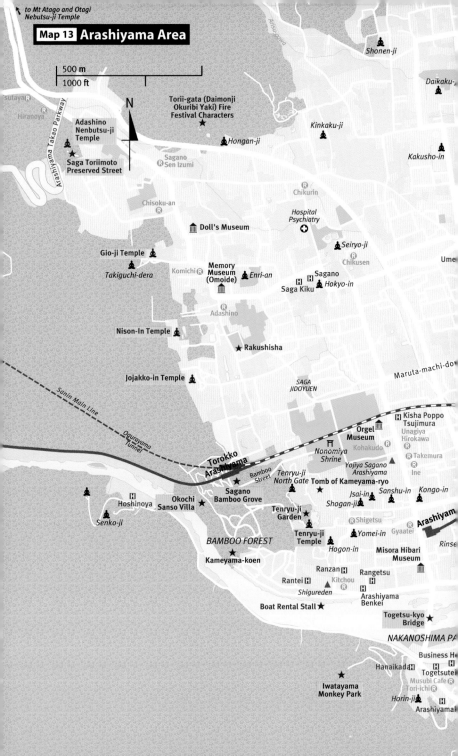

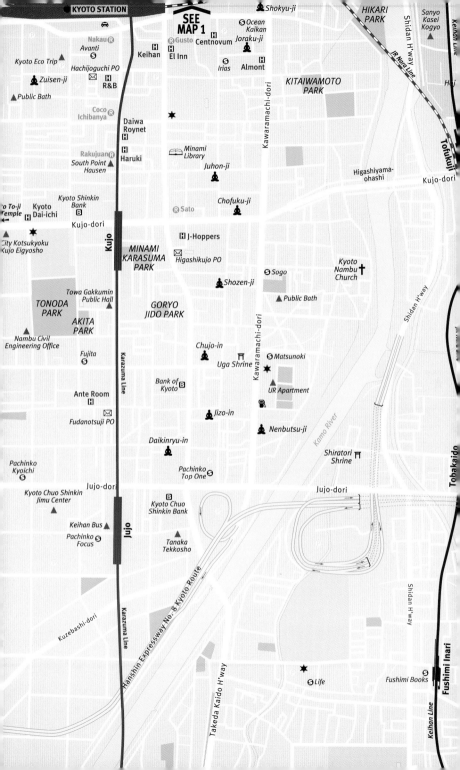

KYOTO STATION

SEE MAP 1

Shokyu-ji

HIKARI PARK

Sanyo Kasei Kogyo

Kenih Line

Nakau

Avanti

Kyoto Eco Trip

Hachijoguchi PO

Zuisen-ji

R&B

Public Bath

Coco Ichibanya

Rakujuan

South Point Hausen

Daiwa Roynet

Haruki

Kyoto Shinkin Bank

Kyoto Dai-ichi

Kujo-dori

o To-ji emple

City Kotsukyoku Kujo Eigyosho

Kujo

Karasuma Line

MINAMI KARASUMA PARK

TONODA PARK

AKITA PARK

Nambu Civil Engineering Office

Fujita

Ante Room

Fudanotsuji PO

Pachinko Kyoichi

Jujo-dori

Kyoto Chuo Shinkin Jimu Center

Keihan Bus

Pachinko Focus

Jujo

Karasuma Line

Kuzebashi-dori

Gusto

Centnovum

El Inn

Keihan

Irias

Ocean Kaikan

Joraku-ji

Almont

Kawaramachi-dori

KITAIWAMOTO PARK

Minami Library

Juhon-ji

Chofuku-ji

Sato

J-Hoppers

Higashikujo PO

Shozen-ji

GORYO JIDO PARK

Towa Gakkumin Public Hall

Chujo-in

Uga Shrine

Bank of Kyoto

Jizo-in

Daikinryu-in

Pachinko Top One

Kyoto Chuo Shinkin Bank

Tanaka Tekkosho

Sogo

Public Bath

Matsunoki

UR Apartment

Nenbutsu-ji

Kyoto Nambu Church

Higashiyama-ohashi

Kujo-dori

Tofukuji

JR Nara Line

Shidan H'way

Hei

Kamo River

Shiratori Shrine

Jujo-dori

Shidan H'way

Shidan H'way

Tobakaido

Hanshin Expressway No. 8 Kyoto Route

Takeda Kaido H'way

Life

Fushimi Books

Fushimi Inari

Keihan Line

Keihan Line

Map 14 **Tofuku-ji and Fushimi-Inari Area**

Imakumano Shrine

Daishindo Books

Korai-ji

Daigo-michi

Shoho-ji

Tsurugi Shrine

Imakuma

Hommachi PO

lic Bath

Kyoto Chuo Shinkin Bank

Kyoto Shinkin Bank

Sansei Hospital

Higashi Oji-dori

Manju-ji

Japan Red Cross Hospital

Seiko-in

Reigen-in   Shorin-ji

iko-an   Kaizo-in

Ryuminan

o-ji   Doju-in   Ritsukyoku-an

Reiun-in   Meian-ji

Ikkain-in

Ryugin-an

Tentoku-in

unda-in   Shumul Honin

esshu-ji   Tofuku-ji Temple

Toko-ji

Keisho-in

Ganjo-ji   Shogaku-an

Nenbutsu-ji   Kenko-in

r Smile   Inariyama Hospital

aka   ne   Komyo-ji

Yomei-in

Nanmei-in

ni Kuno Hospital

Gokuraku-ji

no Hospital

Fushimi Myoken-ji

Yumiya Hachimangu Shrine

Toyakawadaijin

Araki Shrine

Azumamaro Shrine   **Fushimi-Inari Taisha Shrine**

Fushimi Kandakara Shrine

Sokujo-in

Public Bath

Sokusei-in

Kaiko-ji

Hoon-in

Shinzenko-ji

250 m
500 ft

N

Toritonoshinogu

Imakumano Kannon-ji

Nihonsaisho Inaridaimyo Shrine

Reigo-in

Shinshoden

Sennyu-ji Temple

Hiden-in

Daiunin Minamidani Betsuin

Saishokongoin

Sosen-ji

Goshanotaki Shrine

Unryu-in

Kyoto Int'l HS

Chukyotenno Kujo Misasagi

Hanshin Expressway No 8 Kyoto Route

Ennin-ji

Eiko Church

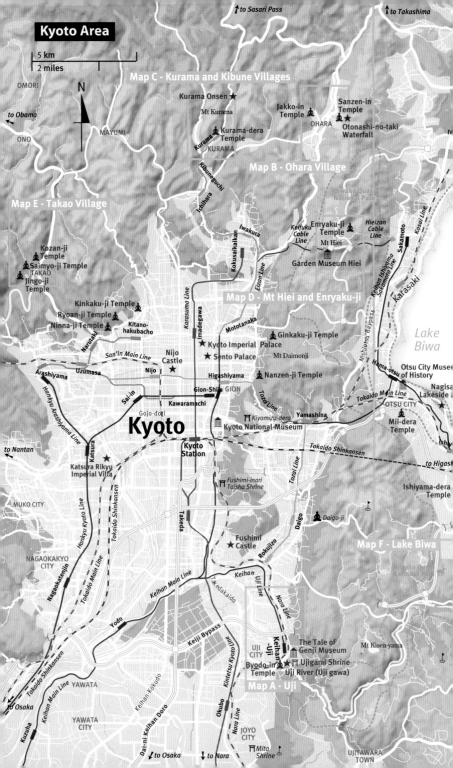

Part 4: MAPS OF KYOTO AREA

Excursions to the Outskirts of Kyoto

If you are spending more than a couple of days in Kyoto, it's a good idea to take a short day trip or overnight trip outside the city. Ringed by mountains on three sides, Kyoto is blessed with relatively little urban sprawl on its outskirts and you can easily reach a pristine mountaintop or picturesque village in an hour or less. Refresh yourself with an excursion if you get fed up with the traffic and crowds. Even though these are sparse compared to Tokyo or New York, they are still traffic and crowds worthy of the seventh largest city in a densely populated country. Where you decide to visit will depend on your goals for the trip.

To hike amid natural surroundings, visit **Mt Kurama** or **Mt Hiei** to the north and northeast of the city. To soak in natural hot springs, head for Mt Kurama or the village of **Ohara**. To enjoy the atmosphere of a small mountain village, go to Ohara or **Takao** (also prime spots for viewing fall foliage during the season—as is the train ride to Kurama). For lake views, visit **Otsu** or other cities alongside Japan's largest lake, **Lake Biwa**. And for temples and historic sites, choose **Uji**, **Mt Hiei** or any of the above for that matter. All of the destinations have major temples, and visiting a temple on a serene mountainside amid natural splendor is altogether different from hitting the well-worn tourist trail in Kyoto city proper. And while the entire Kyoto region has a long history, it's when you get away from the hustle and bustle that it really seems to live and breathe.

Even if you don't have time to take a side trip, if you have a few hours you can enjoy a moderate hike amid unspoiled surroundings and get marvelous panoramic views of Kyoto (and even the skyscrapers of Osaka on a clear day) from **Mt Daimonji** (Daimonji-yama). You can begin the hike at **Ginkaku-ji** (the Temple of the Silver Pavilion), within walking distance or a short bus ride from downtown Kyoto. It takes an hour or so to reach the top of the mountain, which is officially known as Nyoigatake and is nicknamed Daimonji

because it's one of the five mountains on which giant pictograms are set ablaze during the midsummer Daimonji-yaki (or Gozan no Okuribi) Festival; in this case, the kanji character *dai* means "large." You'll walk through the middle of the sacred bonfire site during the hike.

Turn left at the gate of Ginkaku-ji and walk for about a minute toward a stone *torii* gate. Turn right just in front of the gate. Climb the path for a couple of minutes until the path forks, and go right at the fork. The trail is signposted, though signs may not be in English, and is pretty self-explanatory. The hike takes 2–3 hours in all, and you will wind up behind **Nanzen-ji Temple**.

Alternatively, start at Nanzen-ji Temple and look for the picturesque and incongruous brick aqueduct. Follow the road next to the aqueduct toward the mountains and climb the steps until you reach a small shrine (**Nanzen-ji Okuno-in**) with a waterfall. From here, there are multiple trails. Turn left (head north) to reach the summit of Mt Daimonji. See Map 4, pages 50–1, to locate Nanzen-ji and Map 7, pages 56–7, for Ginkaku-ji.

Read on for details about, and maps of, the other destinations.

Enryaku-ji is located on Mount Hiei

Visiting Uji

U ji is a smaller city just south of Kyoto, known for its green tea and cultural treasures and as one of the primary settings of *The Tale of Genji*. Over a millennium has passed since that book was written but, like Kyoto, the city retains many vestiges of its venerable history. It was a favored getaway for Heian-era (AD 794–1192) aristocrats and still makes a serene and scenic day trip from Kyoto.

The best-known attraction is **Byodo-in Temple**, a World Heritage site. Located on the south bank of the Uji River (Uji gawa), its stately Phoenix Hall is pictured on the Japanese 10 yen coin. It has survived intact since 1053 thanks to the pond surrounding it, which protected it from fire and also re-flects the temple enchantingly when still.

Across the Uji River from the temple is another World Heritage site, **Ujigami Shrine**, built around the same time as Byodo-in and recognized as the oldest Shinto shrine in Japan. A short walk from it are several other temples and shrines, and **The Tale of Genji Museum**, featuring multimedia exhibits focusing largely on the final third of the epic novel, known as the Ten Uji Chapters.

The **Uji River** itself is a scenic attraction and you can walk alongside it, taking about an hour to reach **Amagase Dam** before doubling back. A short way up the river, on summer evenings at 7 pm mid-June through mid-September, tourists can enjoy a boat ride and observe the tradition of fishing by torchlight with trained cormorants.

Uji is known throughout Japan for its excellent **green tea**. A package of Uji tea makes a good gift or souvenir and there is plenty to be found at souvenir shops. For a taste of the time-honored tea ceremony, savor a cup at **Taiho-an**, an authentic teahouse next to the river just east of Byodo-in Temple (open 10 am–4 pm).

GETTING TO UJI

From Kyoto Station, the JR Nara Line will be the best option to reach Uji Station, but from the east side of Kyoto the Keihan Line will be easier. The two stations in Uji are not far from one another. From Kyoto Station, it takes 27 min-utes by local train or 17 minutes by express on the JR Nara Line to reach Uji Station (JR). The Keihan Uji Line from Chushojima to Uji Station (Keihan) takes 14 minutes by local train. To reach Chushojima, take the Keihan Main Line from Gion Shijo, Sanjo or Demachiyanagi, about 13 minutes by limited express.

GETTING AROUND UJI

The sights can be reached on foot with ease. See the area map opposite.

Byodo-in Temple

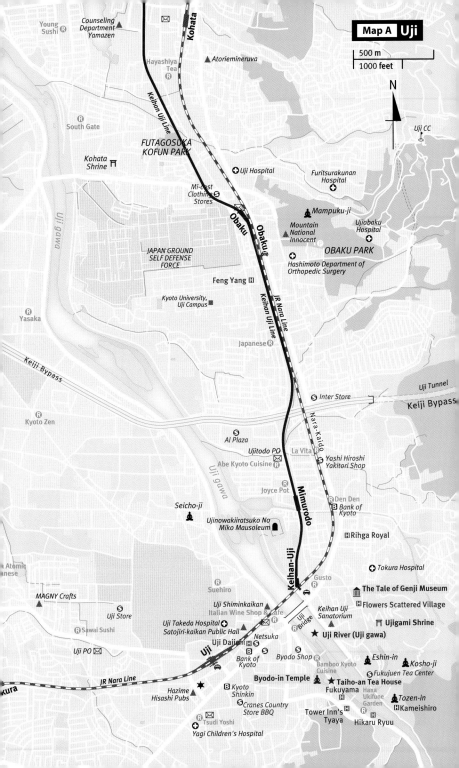

500 m
1000 feet

N

Young Sushi

Counseling Department Yamazen

Hayashiya Tea

Atoriemineruva

Kohata

Keihan Uji Line

Uji CC

South Gate

Kohata Shrine

FUTAGOSUKA KOFUN PARK

Uji Hospital

Furitsurakunan Hospital

Mampuku-ji

Mi-cost Clothing Stores

Obaku

Obaku

Mountain National Innocent

Ujiobaku Hospital

OBAKU PARK

JAPAN GROUND SELF DEFENSE FORCE

Hashimoto Department of Orthopedic Surgery

Uji gawa

Feng Yang

Kyoto University, Uji Campus

JR Nara Line

Keihan Uji Line

Yasaka

Japanese

Keiji Bypass

Inter Store

Uji Tunnel

Keiji Bypass

Kyoto Zen

Nara-Kaido

Al Plaza

Ujitodo PO

La Vita

Yoshi Hiroshi Yakitori Shop

Abe Kyoto Cuisine

Uji gawa

Joyce Pot

Mimurodo

Seicho-ji

Den Den

Bank of Kyoto

Ujinowakiiratsuko No Miko Mausoleum

Rihga Royal

Atomic -nese

Keihan-Uji

Tokura Hospital

Suehiro

Gusto

The Tale of Genji Museum

MAGNY Crafts

Uji Store

Uji Shiminkaikan
Italian Wine Shop & Cafe

Keihan Uji Sanatorium

Flowers Scattered Village

Ujigami Shrine

Sawai Sushi

Uji Takeda Hospital
Satojiri-kaikan Public Hall

Netsuka

Uji Bridge

Uji River (Uji gawa)

Uji PO

Uji Daiichi

Eshin-in

Kosho-ji

-kura

JR Nara Line

Bank of Kyoto

Byodo Shop

Bamboo Kyoto Cuisine

Fukujuen Tea Center

Hazime Hisashi Pubs

Kyoto Shinkin

Byodo-in Temple

Taiho-an Tea House
Fukuyama

Hana Ukifune Garden

Tozen-in

Kameishiro

Cranes Country Store BBQ

Tower Inn's Tyaya

Hikaru Ryuu

Tsudi Yoshi

Yagi Children's Hospital

Visiting Ohara Village

The picturesque rural town of Ohara nestles in a mountain valley north of Kyoto. It's a popular destination for a short trip from Kyoto, especially during the autumn leaf viewing season. This begins in late November in the city, but about a week earlier in the chillier mountains. Even at other times of the year, it's a wonderful place to escape from the hustle and bustle and breathe fresh mountain air, and will certainly be less crowded than at the peak of the leaf changing season.

Sanzen-in Temple is the best-known tourist attraction, with classical gardens, lovely and extensive grounds for strolling and an iconic Ohara sight: benevolently smiling stone statues poking up out of seas of moss. These represent the Buddhist deity Jizo, guardian of the souls of children and the unborn (8.30 am–4 pm, December–February [5 pm March–November]. Entry fee). In the forest behind Sanzen-in is a trail leading to **Otonashi-no-taki**, the "Soundless Waterfall," perfect for an inspiring nature walk.

There are quite a few other temples, the most famous of which is **Jakko-in** (9 am–5 pm). A former nunnery built well over a thousand years ago, it is high up on the more deserted side of the valley opposite Sanzen-in,

and during the season of fall colors its splendid foliage is well worth the climb.

Ohara has natural **hot springs**, which can be bathed in at *ryokan* (inns) or *minshuku* (guest houses) in the town. You can enjoy these not only if you're staying the night, but also if you're on a day trip. They offer lunch and bathing for a set price. Nothing could be better after a few hours of walking (or even before).

GETTING TO OHARA

Kyoto City Bus 17 leaves from Kyoto Station for Ohara every 20 minutes or so (¥580) and takes about 60 minutes. From Shijo Kawaramachi it takes about 45 minutes (¥510). Or you can hop on the Karasuma subway line to Kokusai-kaikan Station (the last station) (about 20 minutes from Kyoto Station, ¥280), then take Kyoto City Bus 19 to Ohara (20 minutes, ¥340, leaving every 40 minutes or so).

GETTING AROUND OHARA

Walking is the way to go. See the area map opposite.

Jakko-in Temple

Map B Ohara Village

↑ to Bomura

500 m
1000 feet

N

Jakko-in Nunnery

Ohara Sanso ⒣

Keitoku-in

Ohara-no-sato ⒣

Ohara-tsuji ⒣

Kusao-Gawa River

Shorin-in Temple (Mondodera)

Hosen-in Temple

Imperial Tombs ★

Ohara Home Village Museum

Jikko-in Temple

Sanzen-in Temple

Tamba-jaya

ⓡ It Sawa

Seryo

Otonashi-no-taki Waterfall ★

Ryoso Chadani ⒣

Bus 19 from Kokusaikaikan Station 20 Mnts
Bus 17 from Kyoto Station 60 Mnts

Gyozan-en ⒣

Jorenge-in

Ohara Kobo

OHARA

⒣ Ono-sanso

Raigo-in Temple

Takano-Gawa River

⒣ Sanzenin-no-sato

⒣ Sanzenin-michi

Villa Uneven Field ⒣

Tamba-jaya

Seshu-in

ⓢ

Ohara Sanzen'in Family

Uenae ⒣

Kitsune ⒣

⒣ Noda-ya

Ohara Memorial Hospital ✚

Takano River

↓ to Kyoto

Visiting Kurama and Kibune Villages

The northern part of Kyoto, known locally as Rakuhoku, largely consists of steep, densely forested mountains, among which lie Kurama and Kibune, both splendid spots for hiking and communing with nature.

Kurama is actually the name of a mountain to the northwest of Kyoto but is also used to indicate the small village around Kurama Station and its environs, which include a hiking course and hot springs. The station is the last one on the Eizan Line, about 30 minutes from downtown Kyoto, and the scenic ride alone itself is well worth the trip. In late November, people pile on the train for a trip through the tunnel of illuminated red maples it passes through on the way. This is quite beautiful in May as well when the maple trees are a fresh spring green.

Outside the station you'll encounter the giant mask of a frightful red goblin with an extremely long nose, representing the powerful Kurama Tengu, believed to dwell here. A god is also said to have descended from Venus several million years ago and alighted on this mountain, another indication of the mystical atmosphere that pervades the place. From the station it's a short walk up the road, with the river on your right, to the main gate of **Kurama-dera Temple**. The temple itself is a short cable car ride up the mountain.

Those looking for a real (albeit not so long) hike can continue along the trail behind the temple to **Kibune**, about an hour with some steep portions. It's another picturesque village with a shrine surrounded by majestic trees. In the warmer months (from May to September), you can dine on chilled noodles served in a unique and dramatic fashion, along with other Kyoto cuisine, at one of several restaurants that serve guests on platforms over a rushing river.

From Kurama Temple, you can come back down via the cable car and head for the hot springs at **Kurama Onsen** (the official name of the spa is Yama no Yado-Mizu no Yado), a few minutes up the road (again with the river to your right) on the right. It costs ¥1,000 to soak in the outdoor natural hot spring bath or ¥2,500 for full access to the outdoor bath, indoor baths, sauna and relaxation area (open 10 am–9 pm [10 pm in winter]).

The above-described course can also be done in reverse, going to Kibune first and then hiking to Kurama and taking the train back from there, though going to Kibune involves taking a bus with a more limited schedule than the train (see below).

GETTING TO KURAMA AND KIBUNE

The Eizan Railway from Demachiyanagi (Keihan Line) to Kurama Station takes 30 minutes (¥410) and leaves every 20 minutes or so.

For Kibune, get off the Eizan Railway at Kibuneguchi Station (27 minutes, ¥410, every 20 minutes), then take the Kyoto bus for Kibune and get off at the Kibune stop (about 5 minutes, ¥160, every 20 minutes between 9.50 am and 4.30 pm). There are no buses in winter (beginning of December through end March).

Kibune Shrine

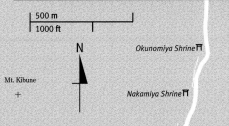

Map C Kurama and Kibune Villages

to Keihokuseryoucho

500 m
1000 ft

N

Mt. Kibune

Okunomiya Shrine

Nakamiya Shrine

to Hanasebesshocho

Mt. Kurama
513m

Kibune Tyaya

Ryokan Ugenta

Kibune Club
And Hiro
Hirobun

Kibune Shrine
Hiroya Ryokan
Torii Tyaya
Ci Pleasure

Mizuura-Yuniwa Garden

Oku-no-in Maoden Shrine

Kibune Fujiya

Kurama Onsen

KIBUNE

Ticket Booth

Sojoga-dani Fudo-do

Kurama Izumi Atsushi

Tatsumi

Kuramayama Museum

Kurama-dera Temple

Tochigiku

Tahoto Pagoda

Osugi-gongen

Yuki Shrine

Tahoto

Beniya

Kiichihogendo

Kuramayama Cable Car

Yoshikura Inari Shrine

Ticket Booth

Sammon

KURAMA

Jizo-ji

Kurama

Aburaya-shokudo

Kurama-so

Keifuku Eizan Line

Yoshuji

Mt. Ryuo-dake

Kibuneguchi

Kibune-Gawa River

Kurama-Gawa

to Gion   *to Keihokuseryoucho*

Visiting Mt Hiei and Enryaku-ji Temple

Northeast of Kyoto stands **Mt Hiei** (Heizan), a sacred and nearly unspoiled mountain that is easily accessible from the city and has a cable car and bus service to the top for those not keen on hiking. Straddling the border between Kyoto and Shiga prefectures, Mt Hiei offers spectacular views of both the city of Kyoto to the west and the shimmering expanse of Lake Biwa, Japan's largest lake, to the east (see pages 84–5).

Near the summit is Hieizan **Enryaku-ji Temple**, usually shortened to just Enryaku-ji. It's a massive temple complex of many halls and pagodas, home to ascetic "marathon monks" who undergo inconceivably rigorous training in pursuit of enlightenment. Enryaku-ji was originally built around AD 800 and grew into a vast and powerful monastery of thousands — too vast for the liking of feudal lord Oda Nobunaga, who burned it down and massacred its inhabitants in the 16th century to eliminate the threat they posed. Enough has been rebuilt for it to be highly impressive nonetheless. Enryaku-ji is divided into three zones: To-do (East Pagoda), Sai-to (West Pagoda) and Yokawa. The most important structures are in To-do, including the head temple Konpon Chu-do, which houses a holy eternal flame that has burned for centuries. The entire complex is worth a stroll around, if time permits. It's pervaded by a solemn spiritual atmosphere, and one can easily understand the Enryaku-ji organization's assertion that the mountain itself and its splendid natural environment are part and parcel of the temple as well.

The other major tourist destination on the peak is **Garden Museum Hiei**, a combination of a museum and Western-style gardens. Although the art on display is nothing to write home about (mainly reproductions of French impressionist masterpieces on ceramic boards, placed on easels in the gardens, which almost seem like an afterthought when surrounded by so much floral splendor), the view from the mountaintop is marvelous and anyone fond of flowers and herbs will not be disappointed.

Those who enjoy a moderate hike may want to climb to the top on foot, starting from Sakamoto Station on the eastern, Shiga Prefecture side of the mountain (the far side from Kyoto). It's a good idea to get started reasonably early as it will take a couple of hours to reach the top, and last admission to the temple is at 4 pm. You may encounter monkeys and other wildlife on the way.

GETTING TO MT HIEI

If planning to hike, take the JR Kosei Line from Kyoto Station to Hieizan-Sakamoto (about 20 minutes). Alternatively, take the Tozai subway line from Sanjo Keihan to Misasagi Station and transfer to the Keihan Ishiyama-Sakamoto Line to Sakamoto (about 40 minutes altogether). From either station, follow the signs for Hiyoshi Taisha Shrine or Cable Sakamoto (about a 20 minute walk from Hieizan-Sakamoto, about 10 minutes from Sakamoto). The JR route is a faster and easier trip from Kyoto but a longer walk to the trailhead once one arrives. The cable car from Sakamoto is another option, letting you enjoy the fabulous view of Lake Biwa at leisure.

If planning to ascend by cable car, however, it would be easier to take the Keihan Main Line to Demachiyanagi (the final station). Transfer to the Eizan Line to Yase-Hieizan-guchi (about 15 minutes, ¥260); unlike the Sakamoto cable car, there is no walk between stations and it doesn't entail going around to the far side of the mountain. From here, take the Eizan Cable Car to the top (¥530 one way/¥1,040 round trip, though it's actually ¥820 one way/¥1,640 round trip, including the final leg of the trip on a ropeway). Cable cars leave every 30 minutes between 8.30 am and 5.30 pm (shortened or extended somewhat in winter and summer).

There are also two buses a day from Kyoto Station to the top of Mt Hiei (Bus 51 departing at 9.25 am and 12.30 pm, about 60 minutes). There are also two buses going back, departing at 12.08 pm and 16.21 pm. These do not run in winter. The advantage is that there are no transfers to deal with, but buses are very infrequent, so careful scheduling is necessary.

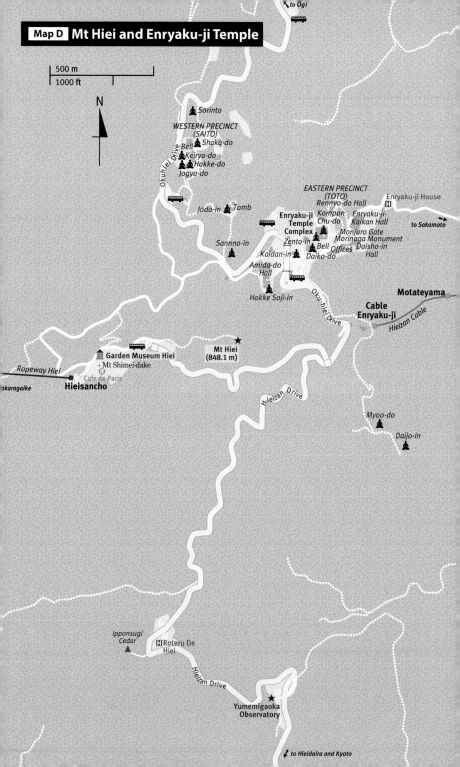

Map D Mt Hiei and Enryaku-ji Temple

to Ogi

500 m
1000 ft

N

Sorinto

WESTERN PRECINCT
(SAITO)
Shaka-do

Bell
Keiryo-do
Hokke-do
Jogyo-do

Okuhiei Drive

EASTERN PRECINCT
(TOTO)
Rennyo-do Hall

Enryaku-ji House

Jodo-in   Tomb

Kompon
Chu-do
Enryaku-ji
Temple
Complex
Zento-in

Enryaku-ji-
Kaikan Hall

Monjuro Gate
Morinaga Monument

to Sakamoto

Sannno-in

Bell
Daiko-do
Kaidan-in
Offices
Amida-do
Hall

Daisho-in
Hall

Motateyama

Hokke Soji-in

Oku-hei Drive

Cable
Enryaku-ji

Hieizan Cable

Garden Museum Hiei

Mt Hiei
(848.1 m)

Ropeway Hiei

+ Mt Shimei-dake
Cafe de Paris
R

akaragaike   Hieisancho

Hieizan Drive

Myoo-do

Daijo-in

Ipponsugi
Cedar

H Roteru De
Hiei

Hieizan Drive

Yumemigaoka
Observatory

to Hieidaira and Kyoto

Visiting Takao Village

Nestled in a mountain valley not far to the northwest of Kyoto, a bit north of Arashiyama-Sagano, is the village of Takao, known throughout Japan as a prime spot for autumn leaf viewing. Rich in history, it has several ancient temples, which are the town's primary tourist destinations. Visiting these temples in their pristine natural environments is an experience altogether different from making the rounds of famous landmarks in downtown Kyoto. Try to avoid weekends during the peak of the fall foliage season (mid-to late November), when the hamlet may be overrun by tourists trying to snap the perfect picture of Japanese maples in all their crimson glory. Visit on a weekday if possible.

Kozan-ji Temple (sometimes written as Kosan-ji) was built on a hillside above the Kioyaki River around AD 1200 and is registered as a World Heritage site. The Japanese maples, older and more massive than in most leaf gazing destinations, mingle with towering ancient cedars. Among the treasures in the temple's possession are the *Choju-giga* (Animal Caricatures) scrolls, which *manga* comics fans may know as "Japan's first *manga*," dating from the 12th to 13th centuries. These are currently on loan to the National Museums in Kyoto and Tokyo but replicas can be viewed, and dedicated *manga* buffs will want to make the pilgrimage. Kozan-ji is also home to Japan's oldest tea plantation, originally planted by a Zen monk who brought back seeds from China and encouraged devotees to ward off drowsiness with the beverage.

Jingo-ji, another impressive temple known for spectacular fall colors, is reached by climbing a long flight of stone stairs. Another flight of stairs leads down to the Kiyotaki River that wends its way through the village. Jingo-ji offers lovely mountain views and the chance to summon good luck by flinging ritual clay tablets from atop a cliff into the river below.

Originally an annex to Jingo-ji, nearby **Saimyo-ji** is smaller but equally picturesque. It's especially known for its charming arched vermilion bridge over the Kiyotaki River. Those averse to climbing stairs will prefer this temple, which also has a pleasant rustic atmosphere and plenty of Japanese maples.

GETTING TO TAKAO

Take Kyoto City Bus 8 from Shijo-Karasuma to Takao (about 45 minutes, ¥500, every 30–60 minutes). This bus is outside the flat fare zone and is not covered by the One-Day Bus Pass. Or take a JR bus from Kyoto Station to Yamashiro-Takao (about 50 minutes, ¥500, every 20–30 minutes). The Yamashiro-Takao stop is closest to Jingo-ji but the bus goes on to Togano-o, which is most convenient to Kozan-ji.

The nearest train station (but not within walking distance) is Saga-Arashiyama on the Keifuku Line. Those who dislike buses, or are staying in the Arashiyama area, may want to take a taxi from Saga-Arashiyama Station (about 10 minutes, about ¥2,000, not a bad deal for a group of several people).

Kozan-ji Temple

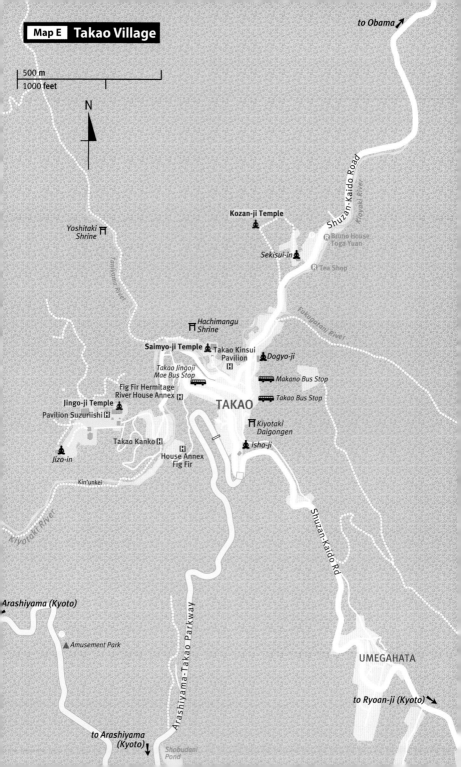

Map E Takao Village

500 m
1000 feet

N

to Obama ↗

Yoshitaki Shrine ⛩

Taniyama River

Kozan-ji Temple 🙏

Kiyotaki River

Shuzan-Kaido Road

Ⓡ *Bruno House Toga Yuan*

Sekisui-in 🙏

Ⓡ *Tea Shop*

Fukugatani River

⛩ *Hachimangu Shrine*

Saimyo-ji Temple 🙏   *Takao Kinsui Pavilion* Ⓗ   🙏 *Dogyo-ji*

Takao Jingoji Mae Bus Stop 🚌   🚌 *Makano Bus Stop*

Fig Fir Hermitage River House Annex Ⓗ   🚌 *Takao Bus Stop*

Jingo-ji Temple Ⓗ   **TAKAO**

Pavilion Suzuriishi Ⓗ   ⛩ *Kiyotaki Daigongen*

Takao Kanko Ⓗ   🙏 *Isho-ji*

🙏 *Jizo-in*   Ⓗ *House Annex Fig Fir*

Kin'unkei

Kiyotaki River

Shuzan-Kaido Rd

Arashiyama (Kyoto)

🔺 *Amusement Park*

UMEGAHATA

Arashiyama-Takao Parkway

to Ryoan-ji (Kyoto) ↘

to Arashiyama (Kyoto) ↓

Shobudani Pond

Visiting Otsu and Lake Biwa

Lake Biwa, the largest freshwater lake in Japan (670 sq km/259 sq miles) and said to be one of the oldest in the world, is named after a traditional stringed instrument (the *biwa*), which has a similar shape. **Otsu**, on its southern shore, is a mid-sized city and the prefectural capital of Shiga, the prefecture to the east of Kyoto. The city proper is not the very best place to behold the natural beauty of the lake, but it is easily accessible from Kyoto, and the lake is large enough to simulate the experience of going to the seaside (without many waves to speak of, however). There is a lakeside park for strolling, cycling or a picnic, some landmark temples, and historical connections to *The Tale of Genji*. Because of Lake Biwa's proximity to Kyoto, Japan's ancient capital, references to Lake Biwa are common in Japanese literature, especially in poetry and in historical accounts of battles.

The author of *The Tale of Genji*, Murasaki Shikibu, is said to have started work on her epic novel at Otsu's **Ishiyama-dera Temple** in 1004. The temple has a period room featuring a life-sized figure of the author at work permanently on display, and occasional special exhibitions on the subject are held. At the other end of the long, narrow city is **Mii-dera**, a larger and equally ancient temple with splendid cherry blossoms in the spring (early April is usually the season for these). The tolling of the evening bell at Mii-dera is one of the "Eight Views of Omi," Omi being the archaic name of the region.

Near Mii-dera are **Otsu Port** and the western end of the 5-km (3-mile)-long **Nagisa Lakeside Park**. Bicycles can be rented at the port as well as at Otsu Station. At the other (eastern) end of the park is **Sunshine Beach**, Otsu's only sand beach, not a stellar swimming spot but a place to relax in good weather. Another way to enjoy the lake is on board the *Michigan*, a replica paddleboat offering dining and entertainment, which leaves from Otsu Port or from the Otsu Prince Hotel four times a day. It may not be to everyone's taste, but could be a fun time for couples or families with kids.

A more picturesque and swimmable beach lies up the western shore of Lake Biwa at

GETTING TO OTSU

The best way to get to Otsu is to take the JR Tokaido Line (bound for Yasu) from Kyoto Station. The journey lasts about 20 minutes and costs ¥190. Trains leave every 5 or 10 minutes.

Alternatively, you can go directly to Ishiyama-dera Temple via the Tozai subway line (bound for Hamaotsu). At Misasagi Station you will have to change to the Keihan Keishin Line to Hamaotsu, then to the Keihan Ishiyama Sakamoto Line to Ishiyama-dera Station (altogether a journey of about 45 minutes, ¥540, leaving every 15 minutes or so).

Omi-Maiko, about 50 minutes from Otsu Station by JR train. Meanwhile, on the eastern side of the lake are other small cities popular for day trips. **Omi-Hachiman**, just over 30 minutes from Kyoto Station, is known for charming canals that can be explored by boat. It also features not only a quaint Japanese-style old town but also older Western-style architecture, a rarity in postwar Japan. Architecture and art buffs will also want to visit the **Miho Museum**, nestled in the mountains south of Lake Biwa about 50 minutes by bus from Ishiyama Station in Otsu. In beautiful natural surroundings, it houses a superb collection of older Western and Asian art in a modernist structure designed by I. M. Pei. Nearby is the town of **Shigaraki**, a ceramics capital most famous for large figures of the droll Tanuki (an indigenous Japanese raccoon dog, portrayed with a large hat, enormous testicles and a flask of saké. Look for these outside restaurants and homes).

Further on up the lake shore, about 45 minutes from Kyoto Station, is **Hikone**, home to **Hikone Castle**, one of the few Japanese feudal castles still surviving intact, and also to the wildly popular feline samurai mascot Hikonyan—a play on the city's name and *nyan*, Japanese for "meow." Hikonyan is credited with sparking the *yurukyara* mascot craze that has been sweeping Japan for years now; most communities and even government ministries are winning hearts and minds with simple yet lovable furry creatures.

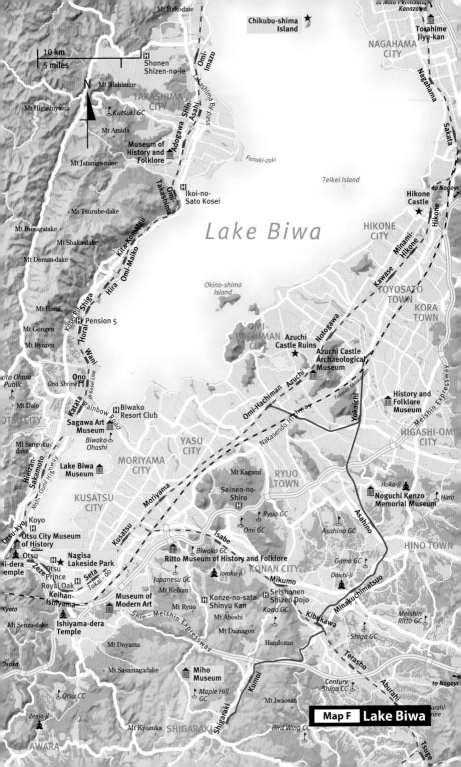

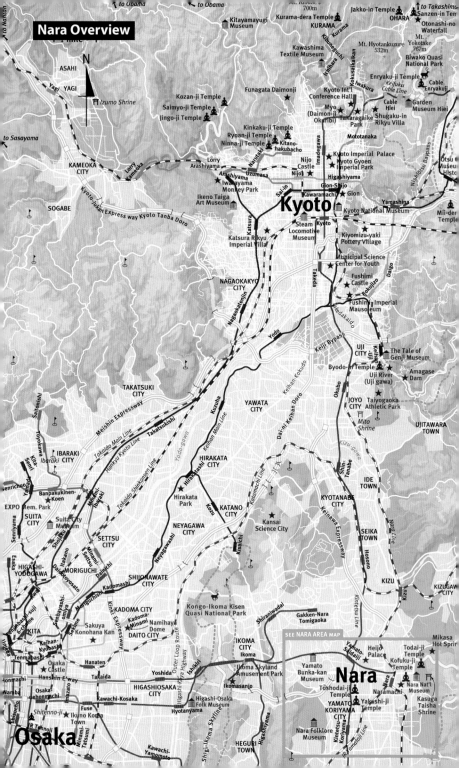

Part 5: MAPS OF NARA

A Visit to Japan's Other Ancient Capital

If you're visiting Kyoto for a week or more, consider taking a day trip to **Nara**, the even more ancient capital just 45 minutes away. While Nara itself is fairly large, most sights are concentrated within walking distance of one another in and around Nara Park (Nara-koen). These include eight temples, shrines and ruins that together constitute the World Heritage site "Historic Monuments of Ancient Nara."

Nara Park is a 20 minute walk from JR Nara Station. You may want to take a bus or taxi instead as you will be doing a lot of walking within the park. The park contains **Todai-ji Temple**, home of the 15-m (50-ft)-tall Great Buddha, the world's largest bronze Buddha; **Kasuga Taisha Shrine**, which has over 1,000 stone lanterns lining the approach, adjoined by the **Kasuga Primeval Forest** and home to the Shinto gods whose messengers are the 1,000 plus deer inhabiting Nara Park; a number of impressive halls and pagodas; and beautiful scenery for strolling. You

can ride around the park by rickshaw for a few thousand yen.

Between JR Nara Station and the park, south of Kintetsu Nara Station, is the historic old town of **Naramachi**. The narrow lanes of this former merchant district are lined with wooden townhouses, many now housing cafés, shops and restaurants. Just wander around or pay a visit to the former merchant residences that are open to the public or the **Harushika Saké Brewery** where you can sample delicious saké originally brewed as a sacrament at Kasuga Taisha Shrine.

Another of Japan's oldest and most celebrated temples, **Horyu-ji**, is a short train ride away. Although a bit of a trek from Nara but of interest to history buffs, is the village of **Asuka-mura**, better known as Asuka. Here you can rent a bicycle to tour its mysterious colossal stones and tombs dating back to prehistory. Another attraction in rural Nara is **Yoshino**, Japan's top cherry blossom viewing destination.

Getting to Nara by Train

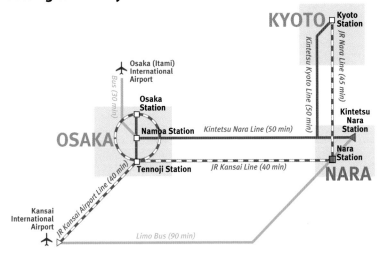

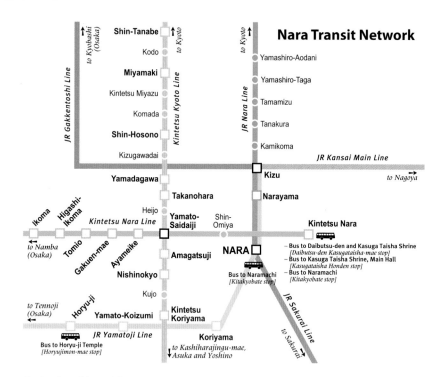

Nara Transit Network

Shin-Tanabe
↑ to Kyobashi (Osaka)
↑ to Kyoto
↑ to Kyoto

Kodo

JR Gakkentoshi Line

Yamashiro-Aodani

Miyamaki

Kintetsu Miyazu

Yamashiro-Taga

Kintetsu Kyoto Line

Komada

Tamamizu

JR Nara Line

Shin-Hosono

Tanakura

Kizugawadai

Kamikoma

JR Kansai Main Line

Yamadagawa

Kizu

to Nagoya

Takanohara

Narayama

Heijo

Ikoma
Higashi-Ikoma
Kintetsu Nara Line
Yamato-Saidaiji
Shin-Omiya
Kintetsu Nara

to Namba (Osaka)
Tomio
Gakuen-mae
Ayameike

– Bus to Daibutsu-den and Kasuga Taisha Shrine
[Daibutsu-den Kasugataisha-mae stop]
– Bus to Kasuga Taisha Shrine, Main Hall
[Kasugataisha Honden stop]
– Bus to Naramachi
[Kitakyobate stop]

Amagatsuji
NARA

Nishinokyo

Bus to Naramachi [Kitakyobate stop]

Kujo

to Tennoji (Osaka)
Horyu-ji
Yamato-Koizumi
Kintetsu Koriyama

JR Sakurai Line
to Sakurai

JR Yamatoji Line
Koriyama

Bus to Horyu-ji Temple
[Horyujimon-mae stop]

to Kashiharajingu-mae, Asuka and Yoshino

Getting To and Around Nara

There are two main train stations in Nara, **JR Nara** and **Kintetsu Nara**. Coming from Kyoto Station, it takes 45 minutes on the JR Nara Line express (¥690). It takes a little under an hour on the Kintetsu Kyoto Line express (¥610). Direct Kintetsu express trains depart hourly. Otherwise, take the train for Kashihara Jingu-mae and change to the Nara-bound train at Yamato-Saidaiji. There are also two Kintetsu limited express trains every hour (35 minutes, ¥1,110).

The JR Line doesn't require changing trains and the Japan Rail Pass can be used. The advantage of the Kintetsu Line is that Kintetsu Nara Station is closer to the sights, being a five minute walk from Nara Park. From the JR station you will have to walk an additional 15 minutes or else take a bus. Go out the central exit of JR Nara station, take a bus bound for Nara-koen (Nara Park) from bus stop 1 and get off at the Kencho-mae stop.

Once you arrive at Nara Park, walking is the best way to get around (see maps, pages 90-3). There are also maps on signboards here and there in the park. Within a full day you can get to all the major sights on foot.

The deer in the park are quite used to people and the bucks have their antlers cut off, so they're no danger though they do occasionally let out odd bleats during the mating season in autumn. Don't feed them anything but the crackers sold by vendors as it could upset their stomachs. Also, be forewarned about groups of schoolchildren at major tourist attractions who approach you to practice their English, apparently on the orders of their teachers. Charming as they are, they may slow down your journey if you stop to answer all their questions, so if you aren't in the mood don't hesitate to tell them politely and cheerfully that you're in a hurry.

If you would prefer not to do a lot of walking, you can take the **Nara Regular Sightseeing Bus** (regular as in regularly scheduled) operated by Nara Kotsu Bus Lines. Every day throughout the year, the bus departs from JR Nara Station at 9 am and from Kintetsu Nara Station at 9.05 am. From around mid-March through the end of November, there are also buses departing at 1.15 pm (JR Nara) and 1.20 pm (Kintetsu Nara). A 3 hour, 40 minute tour (adults ¥3,500, children ¥1,850) of **Historic Monuments in Nara Park** is available. There is also a **Horyu-ji Temple and Nishinokyo Area** tour departing at 10 am or 1.10 pm all year round. If you've already seen the Nara Park area, you might want to consider this option.

Municipal buses can sometimes be useful for getting around to the tourist attractions in Nara (see bus map, page 88), or you can flag a taxi on one of the roads criss-crossing the park if you get tired walking to the station.

The most colorful transport option is the rickshaw, a two-wheeled cart pulled by a runner in traditional Japanese dress. The word rickshaw is derived from the Japanese *jinrikisha* ("human-powered vehicle"). Like horse and carriage rides in New York's Central Park, they're only for the benefit of tourists nowadays. Two people can expect to pay about ¥3,000 per 10 minutes. If pulling a rickshaw looks strenuous to you, consider the fact that it replaced the palanquin (or litter), which lacked wheels and had to be carried.

Aside from Nara Park, the other appealing part of central Nara is the **Naramachi historic district**. Naramachi is a 15 minute walk south of Kintetsu Nara Station or a 20 minute walk southeast of JR Nara Station. You can also take loop Bus 5 or 6 from either train station. With various cafés and restaurants in old converted townhouses, Naramachi is a good place to find a bite to eat in a charming atmosphere. Dining options in and around Nara Park are limited.

While Nara is compact and you can see a lot in a day, those on a longer visit to Kyoto may want to take an overnight trip to Nara.

Accommodation options are similar to those in Kyoto.

If you have extra time, a popular destination outside central Nara is **Horyu-ji Temple**, one of Japan's oldest and most celebrated (8 am–4.30 pm, ¥1,000; JR Yamatoji Line from Nara Station to Horyuji, then a 20 minute walk or 5 minute bus ride). It was built around AD 600 by the legendary Prince Shotoku and is known to every Japanese schoolchild for the famous haiku poem, "I bite into a persimmon/A bell resounds/Horyuji."

Further afield in rural Nara Prefecture is the ancient village of **Asuka-mura** (or simply Asuka), now sleepy farmland but once the Imperial capital of Japan before it was moved to Nara in AD 710 (40 minutes from Kintetsu Nara Station; change trains at Yamato-Saidaiji and Kashiharajingu-mae). Mysterious tombs and colossi date from before the cultural transformations that came with Buddhism and other imports from China. Rent a bicycle outside Kintetsu Asuka Station to explore the countryside for a few hours.

Also famed throughout Japan are the cherry blossoms of **Yoshino**. It gets quite packed with people during the season, early to mid-April, but if you ascend to the observation point, the mountains carpeted with large wild cherry trees in their natural habitat are quite breathtaking, a different experience from the orderly rows of little cultivated trees in the city. It takes almost two hours from Kintetsu Nara to Yoshino Station (change trains at Kashiharajingu-mae).

Todai-ji Temple

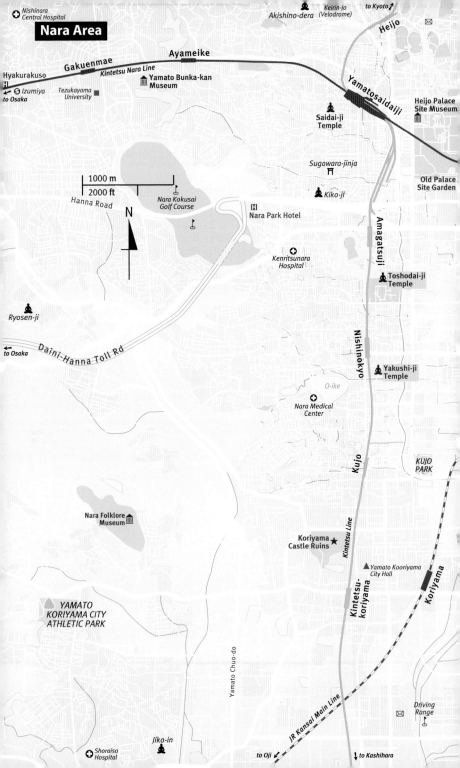

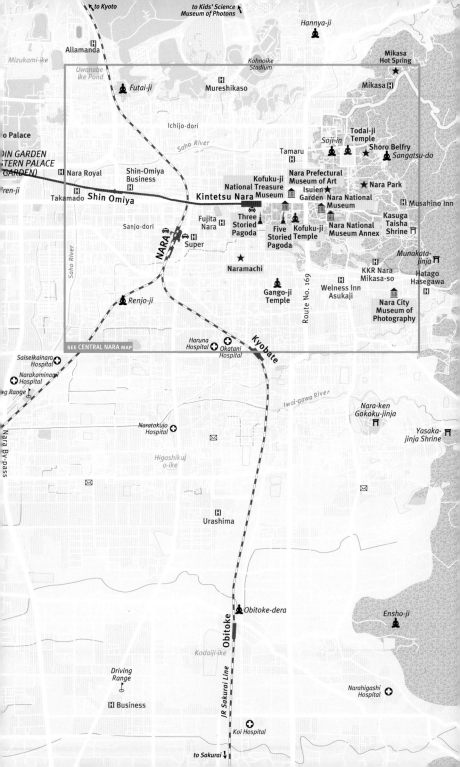

to Kyoto

to Kids' Science
Museum of Photons

Hannya-ji

Mizukami-ike

Allamanda

Mikasa
Hot Spring

Mikasa

Uwanabe-
ike Pond

Kohnoike
Stadium

Futai-ji

Ichijo-dori

Mureshikaso

Soji-in

Todai-ji
Temple

Shoro Belfry

Saho River

Tamaru

Sangatsu-do

o Palace

IN GARDEN
TERN PALACE
GARDEN)

ren-ji

Nara Royal

Shin-Omiya
Business

Kofuku-ji
National Treasure
Museum

Nara Prefectural
Museum of Art

Isuien
Garden

Nara Park

Nara National
Museum

Takamado

Shin Omiya

Kintetsu Nara

Musahino Inn

Fujita
Nara

Three
Storied
Pagoda

Five
Storied
Pagoda

Kofuku-ji
Temple

Nara National
Museum Annex

Kasuga
Taisha
Shrine

Sanjo-dori

NARA

Super

Munakata-
jinja

Naramachi

Hatago
Hasegawa

Saho River

Renjo-ji

Gango-ji
Temple

Welness Inn
Asukaji

KKR Nara
Mikasa-so

Route No. 169

Nara City
Museum of
Photography

SEE CENTRAL NARA MAP

Haruna
Hospital

Okatani
Hospital

Kyobate

Saseikainara
Hospital

Narakominami
Hospital

g Range

Iwai-gawa River

Nara-ken
Gokoku-jinja

Naratokujo
Hospital

Yasaka-
jinja Shrine

Nara By-pass

Higashikuj
o-ike

Urashima

Obitoke-dera

Ensho-ji

Obitoke

Kodaiji-ike

JR Sakurai Line

Driving
Range

Narahigashi
Hospital

Business

Koi Hospital

to Sakurai

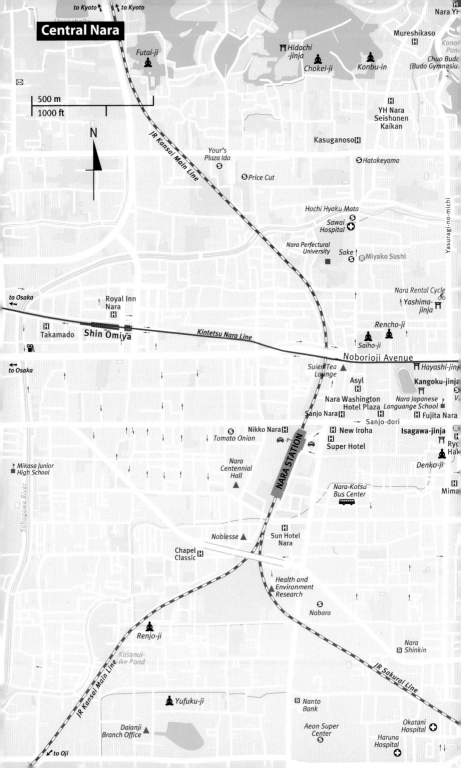

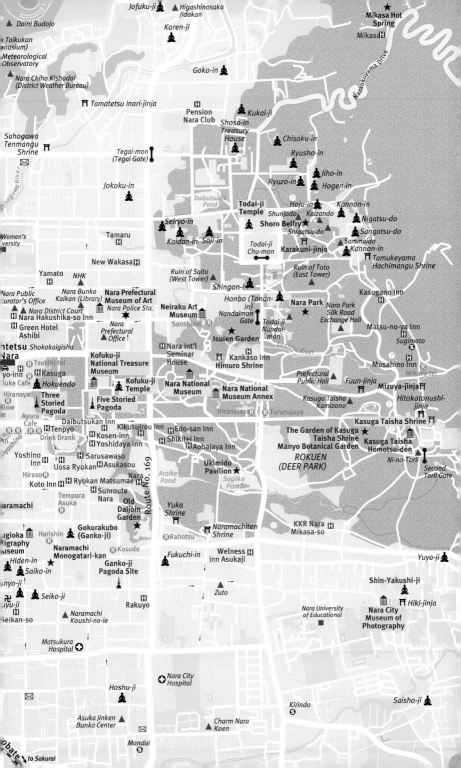

Daini Budojo

Taikukan (nasium)

Meteorological Observatory

Nara Chiho Kishodai (District Weather Bureau)

Jofuku-ji

Higashinosaka Jidokan

Koren-ji

Mikasa Hot Spring

Mikasa

Naraokuyama Drive

Goko-in

Sahogawa Tenmangu Shrine

Tamatetsu Inari-jinja

Pension Nara Club

Kukai-ji

Shoso-in Treasury House

Chisoku-in

Tegai-mon (Tegai Gate)

Ryusho-in

Jokoku-in

Jiho-in

Ryuzo-in

Hogen-in

Daibutsuike Pond

Seiryo-in

Hoju-in

Kannon-in

Todai-ji Temple

Shunjodo

Kaizando

Shoro Belfry

Nigatsu-do

Tamaru

Kaidan-in

Soji-in

Shigatsu-do

Sangatsu-do

New Wakasa

Todai-ji Chu-mon

Karakuni-jinja

Sammaido

Kannon-in

Tamukeyama Hachimangu Shrine

Yamato

NHK

Nara Public curator's Office

Nara Bunka Kaikan (Library)

Nara Prefectural Museum of Art

Ruin of Saito (West Tower)

Kagami ike Pond

Ruin of Toto (East Tower)

Shingon-in

Women's versity

Nara District Court

Nara Hakushika-so Inn

Nara Police Sta.

Neiraku Art Museum

Honbo (Tonan-in)

Nandaimon Gate

Nara Park

Nara Park Silk Road Exchange Hall

Kasugano Inn

Green Hotel Ashibi

Nara Prefectural Office

Sanshotei

Todai-ji Nandai-mon

Matsu-no-ya Inn

Sugimoto

tetsu

Shokokaigisho

Nara

Kofuku-ji National Treasure Museum

Nara Int'l Seminar House

Isuien Garden

Yasukawa River

Musashino Inn

Miharu-tei

Tsukihi-tei

yo-inn

Kasuga

luke Cafe

Hokuendo

Kofuku-ji Temple

Nara National Museum

Himuro Shrine

Kankaso Inn

Prefectural Public Hall

Fuun-jinja

Mizuya-jinja

Hiranoya Willow

Three Storied Pagoda

Five Storied Pagoda

Nara National Museum Annex

Kasuga Taisha Kamizono

Hitokotonushi-jinja

Ayura Cafe

yoshino

Tenpyo

Drink Drank

Daibutsukan Inn

Kikusuirou Inn

Edo-san Inn

Hiranojaya

Turunojaya

Kasuga Taisha Shrine

Yoshino Inn

Kosen-inn

Yoshidaya Inn

Shikitei Inn

Aobajaya Inn

The Garden of Kasuga Taisha Shrine Manyo Botanical Garden

Kasuga Taisha Homotsu-den

Hiraso

Sarusawaso

Uosa Ryokan

Asukasou

Ukimido Pavilion

ROKUEN (DEER PARK)

Ni-no-Torii

Koto Inn

Ryokan Matsumae

Araike Pond

Sagiike Pond

Second Torii Gate

aramachi

Tempura Asuka

Sunroute Nara

Old Daijoin Garden

Yuka Shrine

Yuya-ji

ugioka igraphy useum

Harishin

Kosode

Gokurakubo (Ganko-ji)

Naramachiten Shrine

KKR Nara Mikasa-so

Hiden-in

Naramachi Monogatari-kan

Ganko-ji Pagoda Site

Rahotsu

Fukuchi-in

Welness inn Asukaji

Saiko-in

nyo-ji

Shin-Yakushi-ji

yu-ji

Seiko-ji

Rakuyo

Zuto

Hiki-jinja

Seikan-so

Naramachi Koushi-no-ie

Nara University of Educational

Nara City Museum of Photography

Matsukura Hospital

Nara City Hospital

Kirindo

Saisho-ji

Hoshu-ji

Asuka Jinken Bunka Center

Charm Nara Koen

Mandai

obate

to Sakurai

Index

All maps and diagrams are listed in bold type.

Photo Credits

All photographs in this book have been provided by the author except for those on the pages listed below:

Front cover: © Kobby_dagan/Dreamstime.com
Page 2: © sepavone/Depositphotos.com
Page 4: © Irfan Nurdiansyah/Dreamstime.com
Pages 14, 15: © Tupungato/Shutterstock.com
Page 19 left: courtesy of Taeko Kamei
Page 20: © tupungato/Depositphotos.com
Page 35: © Tupungato/Bigstockphoto.com
Page 36: © Sean Pavone/Shutterstock.com
Pages 37, 76, 82: ©Yasufumi Nishi/© JNTO
Page 38: © Tupungato/Shutterstock.com
Page 41: © JNTO
Page 43: © Lui, Tat Mun/Shutterstock.com
Page 73: © Nicholashan/Dreamstime.com
Page 74: © 安ちゃん/Fotolia.com
Page 78: © JTA /©JNTO
Page 89: ©Nara Prefecture/©JNTO

ABOUT TUTTLE
"Books to Span the East and West"

Our core mission at Tuttle Publishing is to create books which bring people together one page at a time. Tuttle was founded in 1832 in the small New England town of Rutland, Vermont (USA). Our fundamental values remain as strong today as they were then—to publish best-in-class books informing the English-speaking world about the countries and peoples of Asia. The world has become a smaller place today and Asia's economic, cultural and political influence has expanded, yet the need for meaningful dialogue and information about this diverse region has never been greater. Since 1948, Tuttle has been a leader in publishing books on the cultures, arts, cuisines, languages and literatures of Asia. Our authors and photographers have won numerous awards and Tuttle has published thousands of books on subjects ranging from martial arts to paper crafts. We welcome you to explore the wealth of information available on Asia at **www.tuttlepublishing.com**.

Also available from Tuttle Publishing

ISBN 978-4-8053-1213-1

ISBN 978-4-8053-0978-0

ISBN 978-4-8053-1321-3

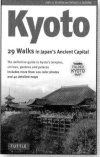

ISBN 978-4-8053-0918-6

ISBN 978-4-8053-1178-3

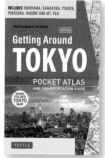

ISBN 978-4-8053-0965-0

ISBN 978-4-8053-1285-8

ISBN 978-4-8053-1208-3

ISBN 978-4-8053-0966-7

Travel Map Japan:
ISBN 978-4-8053-1190-5

Travel Map Tokyo:
ISBN 978-4-8053-1184-4

Travel Map Kyoto:
ISBN 978-4-8053-1185-1

Travel Map Okinawa:
ISBN 978-4-8053-1338-1